EACH MAN SHOULD FRAME LIFE SO THAT AT SOME
FUTURE HOUR FACT AND HIS DREAMING MEET.

—VICTOR HUGO (1802 TO 1885)

 TRAVEL BOOK

NO WORRIES PARIS
A PHOTOGRAPHIC WALKING GUIDE

FIRST EDITION

TEXT BY JERRY SPROUT
PHOTOGRAPHS, ART DIRECTION & DESIGN: JANINE SPROUT
GRAPHIC DESIGN CONSULTANT: MICHAEL SAGUES

With love to Nancy Pettigrew Moser

Merci to John and Anne Strasberg, Ricou, Robert, Hubert, Marinette, Yvon, Claude, Eliette, Andre, Michel, Christian and Cecile Ladrech, Lucy Rozes, Marcelle, Renee and Jean Paolillo, the villagers of Soueich (Haute-Garonne) and Embrousse (Aveyron)

And continued aloha to our Trailblazer ohana, Paula Pennington and Jimmy Dunn, John and Patty Brissenden, Greg Hayes and Joan Wright, Joseph Stroud and Ellen Scott, Rich and Kate Harvey, Linda Kearney, John Manzolati, John and Suzanne Barr, Barbara and Gary Howard, Judy Farnsworth, Dean McKinley, Carol Mallory, Jim Rowley, Elsa Kendall, Edwin O. Hagstrom, Norah Harvey and Greg Hanson, the Rob Moser family, Mark and Vicki Hyde, Tim and Jan Gillespie, the Rickfords—Derek, Anna, Collin, Holly, Owen, Dane and Katie Renee, the Matt Sagues family and Michael Sagues family

Copyright 2012
Printed in Hong Kong. Published in the United States of America

Diamond Valley Company, Publishers
89 Lower Manzanita Drive
Markleeville, CA 96120

Email: trailblazertravelbooks@gmail.com
Website: trailblazertravelbooks.com
Blog: trailblazerhawaii.com

ISBN: 978-0-9786371-6-3
ISBN e-Book: 978-0-9829919-5-4
Library of Congress 2012293502

Base maps: ©MAPS IN MINUTES™ 2011, RH Publications, http://atlasdigitalmaps.com; http://www.mapsinminutes.com, Cornwall, PL33 9EE, United Kingdom.

Proofreader: Gregory Hayes
Cover photo: Trocadero Plaza

Musee Carnavalet

No Worries
PARIS

A PHOTOGRAPHIC WALKING GUIDE

JERRY AND JANINE SPROUT

A Trailblazer Travel Book
DIAMOND VALLEY COMPANY, PUBLISHERS
MARKLEEVILLE, CA

TABLE OF CONTENTS

HOW TO USE THIS BOOK
WALKING TOURS AND PROMENADES

Walking Tours take from a half to full day, depending on your pace, and cover from a few miles to about six miles, varying with detours, stops, and wandering about. Each Walking Tour has its own map. Walking directions are also included in the text. Each tour starts at a Metro stop and ends at another. Generally speaking, the most-famous attractions are in the lower-numbered tours.

The **Promenades** are shorter in length, taking about a half-day. Most of these excursions begin and end at the same Metro stop, usually farther out from the center of the city. Walking directions are included, although Promenades are more wandering about than following a set route.

No Worries Paris takes readers on a tour of the city, to virtually all the famous and historic sites, and quirky places—all of them along the most visually stunning route possible.

Postcards, listed at the beginning of each tour, are the most well known places, as well as the ones likely to be remembered. Of course, memorable places are numerous in Paris, too many to be mentioned in Postcards, let alone in the text of the book. Keep your senses keened, and you may see ten percent of what there is to see as you stroll on by. These walks still yield new experiences after many repetitions.

The **Thumbnail** gives a brief summary of the atmosphere and character of the walk. In the briefest of terms, it tells you where you're going. The **Big Picture** gives tips for each Walking Tour—perhaps the best time and day to visit, ways to shorten the tour or connect with others, and suitability for kids.

WALKING TOUR CONTENT
No Worries Paris leads the way with photographs, text, and maps. The opening photographs are the **Coming Attractions** for the entire Walking Tour. The photos that follow the maps at the start of the written content are illustrative of nearby text. Each photo is captioned. Photo content is indexed.

Following the tour's map is a paragraph of **street directions**, which mirror the green route shown on the map. The content that follows refers to the area described in the preceding directions. Then comes another paragraph of directions, followed by its related content. People and places of interest are boldfaced. **Background and brief histories** are given, especially for the places listed as Postcards.

No Worries Paris also notes the hangouts for writers, painters, actors, and other artists from America and around the globe and over the centuries. The text will note if a visit to a particular attraction or museum is included in the time allotted for the Walking Tour: some places, like the Louvre, Tour Eiffel, and Musee d'Orsay require days unto themselves.

The content for the Promenades is similar to the Walking Tours: walking directions are followed by boldfaced proper names.

The idea of *No Worries Paris* is to get to know the city by actually seeing it on foot, using the most photogenic routes possible. It takes lifetimes to "know" Paris, and even then, good luck. But walking around the entire place will give anyone an unforgetable first impression. To do all of the walks in this book at a reasonable-but-not-frenetic pace would take three or four weeks.

GETTTING AROUND PARIS
LAY OF THE LAND
Paris is oval-shaped, roughly seven miles across, encircled by a freeway (Boulevard Peripherique) and split east-to-west by the River Seine. Twenty neighborhoods (*arrondissements*, each divided further into

four *quartiers*) spiral outward from the small island in the center of the city (Ile de la Cite). Recorded history dates from about 300 BC. Urban hikers, if so inclined, can make it anywhere on foot in a day. On the other hand, a single locale can easily absorb a day's worth of curiosity.

All of Paris is well trod. If a single footprint could be allotted one-quarter inch in height, then all the individual footprints trod at Tour Eiffel or Notre Dame for just one year, if stacked, would create a pinnacle nearly forty miles high. And yet, given the intricacy of the city, no two wanderings ever are likely to be the same. Paris delivers the grand sense of place that is dreamily anticipated, and yet also manages to yield a surprisingly personal experience. A seven-story height limit on buildings and plenty of wide-open spaces make the famous attractions visible from afar, sticking out like cartoon drawings.

LODGING
Paris is dotted with hotels, all using a star system as a rating. In general, rooms will be smaller than comparably priced rooms in the U.S. Another lodging option is to rent a furnished apartment from an agency. You will normally get more space for the money, including kitchens and washer-dryers (though scaled down in size). One good and reputable agency is vacationinparis.com. Preview all their listings online and check for availability. They'll send you the keys before you leave. When buying a room online, be sure to verify the reputation of the agent.

FROM THE AIRPORT
Paris has two major airports: Charles de Gaulle and Orly. If the flight times and price work for you, Air France has excellent meals and service. When booking with any airline, try for a nonstop flight, which saves much time and energy. The RER trains serve both airports and make frequent stops in Paris. Cabs are also available, for about 50 to 60 dollars, not bad if you have several people in your group. Air France also runs a bus to Paris, with departures every 15 minutes and prices around 20 dollars. The catch is that it stops only at Place Charles de Gaulle (Arc de Triomphe) and near l'Opera at Rue Scribe. Unless your hotel is near these places, you'll have to take the Metro or cab from there.

Another good option is to book an airport shuttle before you leave. The price will be less than a cab, and the convenience will be a godsend when getting to your accommodation after a long day of travel. A number of shuttles are listed online. One usually reliable service is airportconnection.com. You can pay for and confirm your ride before leaving home.

THE METRO
Connecting everyplace in Paris to every other is a warren of more than a dozen different Metro lines with several hundred stations, some aboveground but mostly below. Several train lines (the RER) also transect the city, its stations and tickets interchangeable with those of the Metro.

With a single ticket, riders can pop down any Metro and pop up at another, though often having to take walkways and stairs to connect with other lines. Connecting lines (*correspondence*) are color-coded and well-signed. The sign for each line always lists the last stop for the line in the direction you are heading. Metro cars run every few minutes, less frequently on weekends.

Tickets are good for all connections, even if you exit (*sortie*) for about an hour and come back. Visitors will save money by buying a string of 10 tickets, called a *carne*. If you are staying for more than a week, and may use the Metro for more than one round-trip per day, consider purchasing *Passe Navigo Decouverte*. It's available at larger Metro stops and RER stations. This transit card allows for unlimited travel on buses, Metro, and trains in Paris. It employs a magnetic strip to be swiped over a reader at the turnstile, which works even if the card is on the outside pocket of a purse or wallet. Cards are good for a week (or a month), but must be purchased on a certain day of the week, normally Fridays. Once you buy the card, it can be recharged and used again. A passport-type photo is required; most stations have photo booths (see www.ratp.fr/).

Tourists can also go online before visiting and buy a *Paris Visite* pass, which also is good for the RER, Metro, and buses. It comes with various options, including number of days needed and travel outside central Paris. Prices are somewhat higher than *Passe Navigo Decouverte*, but you can buy the *Visite* online before leaving, and it is not keyed to a Friday purchase. Discounts at museums are included.

STREET GEAR

For footwear, fashion follows function: make sure you bring something that will walk comfortably over concrete, stairways, and cobblestones. Most visitors will want to carry their passport, map, books, camera, phone, water bottle and whatever other personal stuff. You may want to avoid a backpack, and opt instead for a shoulder bag or book bag with zippered pockets. The shoulder bag keeps all your valuables in front of you, which is safe, convenient, and maneuverable in tight spaces. In museums, you will most often be required to check a backpack, while you can keep a shoulder-style bag with you.

PEEING IN PARIS

Paris is not for the weak of bladder. Using a restroom is not an entitlement. Unless using the facilities at a restaurant after a meal, you will need to be resourceful. Good news is that the famous stand-alone toilets on street corners are now free. The bad news is that fewer of them exist. Other options are Starbucks, McDonalds, and other American chains. The pee-at-will philosophy has come across the pond with the brand names. The foyers of museums (you can normally get in for free to get to the gift shop) are also likely places to find an available restroom. Parks and churches will often have toilets, funky though they may be, especially the former. Department stores are often pay-to-pee, but many will consider this a value.

A must-pee: The Toilettes de la Madeleine are off to the the side of the church's front steps. A discrete sign marks stairs that descend to an Art Nouveau-decorated world of carved wood and gleaming porcelin. A small fee is charged.

STREET SMARTS

Street violence is almost unheard of in Paris, in spite of its revolutionary history. Van loads of police, smartly dressed in Navy helmets, sweaters, and pads, are parked about at the ready. Small squads of military men toting machine guns sometimes patrol tourist zones. Thieves are common enough, however, and you should keep an eye on your stuff. Street hucksters are also around, often teenaged "gypsy" girls, who will approach with a well practised tale of woe, intent on ridding you of spare money. If someone approaches and asks if you speak English, the best answer is usually, "no." Paris does have a few punks, who vandalize with spray cans (as opposed to real grafitti artists) and entertain themselves by verbally abusing tourists—and everyone else. These guys are infrequently at train stations and in the outer neighborhoods. Not a big problem.

MAP FOR AN UNPARALLEL WORLD

The maps in *No Worries Paris* work for the walks, but you should have a back up. Two excellent choices are: The Paris Mapguide, by Michael Middleditch; and Paris Plan by Michelin). In both books, maps are arranged contiguously, rather by arrondissement, which makes it easy to flip around.

PARLAY VOO FRANSAY

Speaking French is not as important as it once was for getting around. There are millions of tourists and you will frequently hear English and other languages. The Euro and ATMs have made it much easier to make transactions. Internet devices and smart phones aid in finding things. Many Parisians, particularly the younger people, speak some English. As mentioned above, the Metro is well signed and color-coded, making it easier to navigate for Americans than it is to get around most U.S. cities.

Still ... you'll want to be able to speak a few phrases. Millions of people are walking around Paris having a zillion conversations. Parisians punctuate their interactions consistently with a few phrases of politeness, which keep order and show respect. Start with hello, end with good-bye and thank you, and use pardon or excuse me in between when appropriate.

When entering a store, or addressing anyone for that matter, say 'Good Day, Sir (or Madame). Not to do so is impolite and you may be then greeted with the famous French freeze. Though, even if your manners are impeccable, do not expect a salesperson or waiter (do not call them *garcon*, use *monsieur*) to be overly friendly. They won't be all smiles and ask if you if you found everything alright today or if you need help out (let alone bag your purchases), and certainly will not say, "Hi, my name is Jean Paul and I will be your waiter today." Reserved politeness rules the day.

In situations where customer service is required, don't expect that you will be right. If you have a problem, in most cases it's your problem. The stereotype of the haughty male waiter does a have basis in reality. These guys are pros and being cheery is not part of their culinary skill set. But people on the street are generally friendly, and in the end Paris is like most places: doors open more often when visitors show respect, interest, and decent manners.

Good day or Hello, *Bonjour* (bon-zhoor)
Always follow this greeting with:
Mister or Sir, *Monsieur* (muh-syuh)
Madame, *Madame* (mah-dahm)
Miss, *Mademoiselle*
Excuse me or I'm sorry, *Excusez-moi*
(ex-koo-zay mwah)
Thank you, Merci (mare-see)
You're welcome, *De rien* (dah ree-ehn)
Please, *S'il vous plaît* (seel voo play)
Yes, *Oui* (wee); No, *Non* (nong)
Good-bye, *Au revoir* (oh ruh-vwar)
Good evening, *Bonsoir* (bon-swar)
OK, *d'Accord* (dah-core)
Excuse me, I do not speak French
Excusez-moi, je ne parle pas français (Ex-koo-zay mwah, zha nuh pahrl pah frhun-say)

FOOD

Eating all meals at a leisurely pace leaves little time in the day for walking around. A compromise is to eat street food during the day. Street food in Paris is not fast food. You will pass by curbside vendors and store windows resplendent with foodstuffs that will need no translation. Crepes, commonly filled with sweet stuff, are commonplace, cooked at a window that opens to the sidewalk. A bistro, café, or *brasserie* with food to go will usually be signed *a emporter*. For off-beat restaurants that are easy on your budget, check out www.doitinparis.com.

Every *quartier* has a cluster of food shops. Some outdoor markets occur on particular days, but many streets host a non-moveable feast. Most of the best market streets in Paris are described in the Walking Tours:

Rue Mouffetard (WT2); Rue de Buci (WT3); Place de la Madeleine (gourmet shops) (WT4); Rue Montorgeuil (WT5); Marche Enfants Rouge (WT6); Marche d'Aligre (WT7); Rue Lepic and Rue des Martyrs (WT9); and Rue Cler (Promenade One).

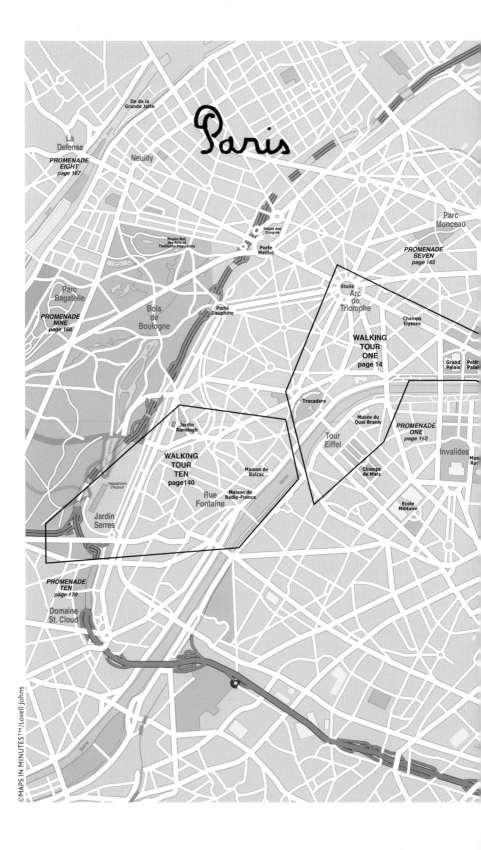

Paris

Île de la
Grande Jatte

La
Défense

Neuilly

Parc
Monceau

Palais des
Congrès

Musée Nat.
des Arts et
Traditions Populaires

Porte
Maillot

Étoile
Arc
de
Triomphe

Champs
Elysees

Parc
Bagatelle

Bois
de
Boulogne

Porte
Dauphine

WALKING
TOUR
ONE
page 14

Grand
Palais

Petit
Palai

Trocadero

Musée du
Quai Branly

Invalides

Mus
Roc

Jardin
Ranelagh

Tour
Eiffel

WALKING
TOUR
TEN
page140

Maison de
Balzac

Champs
de Mars

Hippodrome
d'Auteuil

Rue
Fontaine

Maison de
Radio-France

Jardin
Serres

Ecole
Militaire

Domaine
St. Cloud

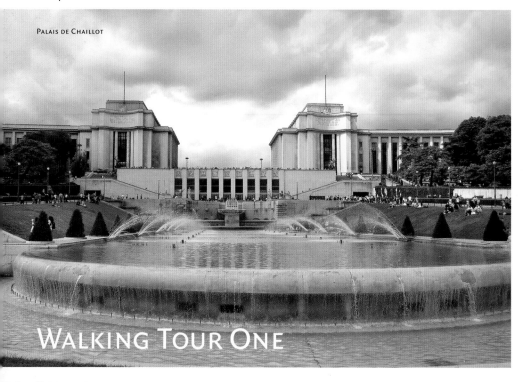

PALAIS DE CHAILLOT

WALKING TOUR ONE

POSTCARDS:

Trocadero Plaza and Palais de Chaillot ... Tour Eiffel ... Champs de Mars ... Ecole Militaire ... Musee Branly ... Avenue Georges V ... Arc de Triomphe ... Champs Elysees ... Grand Palais and Petit Palais ... Pont Alexandre ... Jardin des Tuileries ... Musee du Louvre

THUMBNAIL:

Walking Tour One, along the major monuments of Paris, is the perfect way to spend day one after being cooped up in an airplane. The grand scale of the city is revealed from wide-open formal parks. First-time visitors will see many of the major sites, and Francophiles will become reacquainted.

BIG PICTURE:

You could spend a week making the worthwhile stops of the walking tour. For that matter you could spend a week at the Louvre. But you can also spend one long day with enough time to dip in here and there for stops—and come away with a grand sense of place. This walk is also easy to navigate. For a more leisurely pace, Walking Tour One, can be divided into two days: Spend the first day around the Eiffel Tour, and instead of crossing the river to Avenue George V, continue by seeing the sights of Promenade One, page 152, which is adjacent to the Eiffel. On day two, start at the Arc de Triomphe and take in the Louvre.

DISTANCE: 5 TO 6 MILES   TIME: 4.5 TO 8 HOURS

PETIT PALAIS

CHAMPS DE MARS

PONTE ALEXANDRE

CHAMPS ELYSEES

ARC DE TRIOMPHE

TUILERIES

TUILERIES

PLACE DE TROCADERO

MUSEE BRANLY

WALKING TOUR
One

START AT TROCADERO METRO STOP ON LINE 9

WITH THE STATUE OF WWI'S MARSHAL
FERDINAND FOCH ON HORSEBACK POINTING
THE WAY FROM PLACE DU TROCADERO,
MARCH UP THE WIDE STAIRS TO THE PARVIS
(PLAZA) OF PALAIS DE CHAILLOT.

From the plaza is one of the monumental
views for which Paris is famous: You look
from the center of the Trocadero, across
the Seine through the Tour Eiffel and
beyond to the Champs de Mars and Ecole
Militaire—all laid out in perfect symmetry.
The wide-open space of the parvis was
once filled by the **Palais de Trocadero**,
built in 1878 for a world exposition and
then torn down. The palace was named
for a village that previously occupied
the hilltop. A roving crew of tiny-tower
and trinket salesmen provide today's
commerce.

The twin curved buildings to either side
of the space are the neo-classical **Palais
de Chaillot**, museums that date from
the 1937 Paris Exhibition. To your right
as you face the Tour Eiffel is the **Musee
de l'Homme** (under renovation until
2013), which depicts human history from
caveman times. The matching wing on the
left is the **Musee Cite de l'Architecture
et du Patrimoine**, an airy (23,000 square
meters) display of architectural molds from
medieval times to present day. Though the
collections are excellent—and the interiors
of the palace afford inspiring views of the
Tour Eiffel—you will probably want to save
a visit for another day.

GO DOWN THE STAIRS (LEFT OR RIGHT) AND
CROSS THE BRIDGE (PONT D'IENA) TO TOUR
EIFFEL.

Before reaching the river, you will pass
through **Jardins du Trocadero**, which

feature bronze statues of Apollo and
Hercules, and the **Aquarium du Trocadero**.
A fountain with two-dozen jets squirts
bursts toward the Eiffel. Across the bridge,
steps lead to a broad quay, one of the ports
for river-touring boats (Bateaux Parisiens),
and a spot where many tourists take a
break.

Perhaps the world's most beloved and
recognized structure, the **Tour Eiffel** was
not received warmly by most Parisians
when it was built as part of Exposition
Universalle in 1889. Some 300 artists and
civic leaders signed a petition of protest.
Later, novelist Guy de Maupassant used
to lunch on top, since it was "the only
place in Paris where I don't have to see
it." Colleague Alexandre Dumas called
the "hollow candlestick" a "work of
uselessness." Gustave Eiffel, who also
designed the framework for the Statue of
Liberty, won a contest among engineers
to build a tower of 1,000 feet, which was
nearly twice as high as the Washington
Monument, then the world's tallest. A
communications tower on top brings
today's height to 1,063 feet, the tallest
structure in Paris. It was scheduled to be
torn down and scrapped after 20 years,
but meteorologists and communications
scientists won a plea to let it stand.

Find a spot amid digital shutterbugs
directly underneath the tower and look
up to behold the stats: Under Eiffel's
direction, some 300 workers labored for
two years (incurring zero fatal accidents)
to assemble 18,000 pieces of prefabricated
iron lattice weighing a total of 10,000
tons with more than 2.5 million rivets.
The project came in under budget and a
week early. It is the world's most-viewed
attraction with nearly 300 million visitors,
coming these days at a rate of ten million
per year. The first level is at 187 feet, the

second at 377 feet (these two reachable via stairs), and the top is lofted at 899 feet—where wind sways the structure up to five feet.

TIPS FOR VISITING TOUR EIFFEL: Given the essential sights on the remainder of this walk, you'll probably want to save an ascent for another day. To avoid lines and save time, arrive a little before it opens, normally at 9:30. It's cheaper and faster, given the lines, to walk the first two levels, which takes about 15 minutes. If you want to go to the top, you can buy an elevator ticket in addition to the stairway ticket (at the south tower). To ride all the way to the top (you have to get out at the second level anyway), use the east tower ticket booth. Don't miss the cinema and museum on the first level. The second level is ringed by two viewing decks, and the height is just right to check out the sights of the city, laid out like a 3D model. Since Paris has a seven-story height limit on buildings, the well-known monuments are plainly visible. Many people will want to reach the top as a matter of principle, but the airborne view is less intimate. At night, on the hour, Tour Eiffel turns into a light show. Closing time can be as late as midnight, varying with the season.

CONTINUE AWAY FROM THE TOWER ACROSS CHAMPS DE MARS TOWARD ECOLE MILITAIRE.

Champs de Mars was originally a parade ground and training area for the national military school, **Ecole Militaire**, which was founded in 1751. France's fabled Emperor Napoleon Bonaparte studied here for three years to be an artillery officer in 1784, when he was a fresh from the provinces as a young gentleman without means. During five world exhibitions from 1867 to 1937, the walkways and kempt gardens of today were a bedlam of buildings and the flotsam

of events. The first hydrogen balloons rose here in the late 1700s—the inspiration for Jules Verne's novel. The restaurant in the Tour Eiffel bears his name.

HEAD BACK TOWARD THE TOWER, PASS TO THE RIGHT, AND CONTINUE TOWARD THE RIVER. JUST BEFORE QUAI BRANLY, TURN RIGHT ON A BIKE PATH THAT PARALLELS THE BUSY STREET.

A tall glass palisade shelters the modernistic **Musee du Quai de Branly** from the road. A walkway spirals through gardens to the entrance. Inside are artifacts from the native cultures of Asia, Oceania, Africa, and America.

IN FRONT OF THE MUSEUM, CROSS THE FOOTBRIDGE PASSERELLE DEBILLY. AT AVENUE DE NEW YORK, WALK DOWN THE STAIRS AND WALK ALONG THE QUAY TO THE NEXT BRIDGE (PONT DE L'ALMA). WALK UP AND CROSS THE AVENUE.

Across the busy avenue is an unofficial **shrine to Princess Diana**, the gold-leafed Flame of Liberty, a full-sized replica of that atop the Statue of Liberty. Diana's fatal accident in 1997 took place in the Alma Tunnel, just across from the *place*.

WITH THE RIVER AT YOUR BACK, GO AROUND THE LEFT SIDE OF PLACE DE L'ALMA, AND CONTINUE UP AVENUE GEORGE V ON THE LEFT SIDE TO AVENUE DES CHAMPS ELYSEES.

Swank Avenue **George V** exudes French flair, laced with many ties to 20th century American history. On the left as you begin is fashion house **Yves Saint Laurent**, famous for putting clothes on beautiful women, while across the street is **Crazy Horse**, a nightclub just as famous for taking them off. Gothic **American Cathedral** is at #23, where throngs attended Gertrude Stein's funeral in 1946 and where weekly services, known for splendid music, play to a packed house. Next up is elegant **Hotel George V**. Visitors are allowed inside to view superlative floral displays, without, let's hope, raising the ire of a haughty concierge—such as depicted in the Megan Ryan-Kevin Cline movie *French Kiss*, which was filmed here. In 1933, the hotel was a favorite of jazz great Duke Ellington. Across the avenue, just as you reach the Champs Elysees, is the café **Le Fouquet**, opened in 1899 and known in its early years as a hangout for Irish writer James Joyce (simple eater, big tipper), an icon in France. The café was a front-row seat for the WWII liberation of Paris parade and became a post-war haunt for American journalists, notably Art Buchwald. As plaques and photos attest, the well-heeled glitterati have included Chaplin, Chevalier, Roosevelt, Churchill, and Jackie O. More current celebs arrive at Le Fouquet when it hosts the yearly Cesar awards, the French equivalent of the Oscars.

GO LEFT ON THE CHAMPS ELYSEES TO PLACE CHARLES DE GAULLE. CROSS THE AVENUE TO YOUR RIGHT AND THEN TAKE THE UNDERGROUND PASSAGE TO THE ARC DE TRIOMPHE.

After winning the Battle of Austerlitz in 1806, Napoleon ordered the building of the **Arc de Triomphe** to honor the valor of his Great Army. But it was not completed for 30 years—and when his body was brought home from his final exile in St. Helena in 1840, the Emperor became the honoree of what was the first of many national events to be staged here. Inspired by the King Louis Philippe bas-reliefs adorning the

SEINE, PASSERELLE DE BILLY

CHAMPS ELYSÉES FROM ARC DE TRIOMPHE

TOP, ARC DE TRIOMPHE

Sortie
Exit
Salida

CAFÉ MARLY, LOUVRE

164-foot high span, beloved author Victor Hugo affectionately called it "a heap of glory." Perhaps the most glorious event here was Hugo's funeral in 1885. A Tomb of the Unknown Soldier, dating from 1920, lies beneath the structure. Formerly a grassy hilltop, the site in 1970 was named Place Charles de Gaulle, though most Parisians still refer to it as Etoile (the Star), a reference to the 12 avenues that radiate out from the *place.*

The **Arc de Triomphe** normally is not crowded and a trip to the top is almost essential. You can ride a tiny elevator or take a dizzying spiral staircase. An admission is charged. From the top is the grand monumental view that for many defines modern Paris. One angle is down the middle of the Champs Elysees, through the center of Place de la Concorde and Jardin des Tuileries, and through the apex of the glass pyramid at the Louvre. Opposite that is the view up the center of Avenue Charles de Gaulle to the monolithic Grande Arche at La Defense. It's about six miles from La Defense to the Louvre, called the **Axis Historique**.

BACKTRACK FROM THE ARCH THROUGH THE PASSAGE AND CONTINUE DOWN THE CHAMPS ELYSEES.

With charm-free fast-food outlets, cineplexes, interior malls, and megastores, the **Champs Elysees** may be pegged by visitors as being famous simply for being famous. Certainly, the 50-foot wide sidewalks are built to hold the tens of thousands who have gathered for the many famous processions—among them the student marches of the late 1960s and the yearly finale for the Tour de France bicycle race. The route was first ploughed through the swamps and fields in 1616 on orders of Queen Marie de Medici, who wanted

a parkland made of the hillock at today's Etoile. The rough, nearly two-mile route was extended northwesterly in 1724 to Pont Neuilly, to lend symmetry to the Tuileries, but it was still a backwater for ruffians until sidewalks and streetlights were added in the mid-18C, during the Second Empire of Napoleon III.

Café life thrives amid commerce on the upper end of the "Glorious Way." Notable are the Drug Store near the arch and the Lido cabaret on the left past Rue Balzac. Of interest to Americans: Just past Lido, 3 Rue de Berri is where Helen Keller lived and wrote her autobiography.

CROSS AROUND ROND POINT (WHERE SIX AVENUES CONVERGE AT A FOUNTAIN) AND VEER LEFT INTO THE PARK. THEN DOUBLE-BACK AND CROSS CHAMPS ELYSEES ON AVE. WINSTON CHURCHILL. CONTINUE ON TO PONT ALEXANDRE.

Past Rond Point, the avenue becomes parkland with statuary all the way to Place de la Concorde—**Jardins des Champs Elysees**. The park was a childhood playground for Marcel Proust, and near where (at 1 Avenue de Marigny) John Steinbeck rented "a pretty little house, right in the center of Paris."

On the right, when walking down Avenue Churchill is the aptly named **Grand Palais**, with majestic floral reliefs, a classical stone façade, and a roof adorned at its corners by flying chariots and horses. The palace was built for the 1900 Universal Exhibition, and now features the city's blockbuster art exhibits. Behind this building is **Palais de la Decouverte**, since 1937 a museum for students of the sciences.

On the other side of the avenue is the **Petit Palais**, another lavish example of

VIEW FROM PONT ALEXANDRE

JARDIN DES TUILERIES

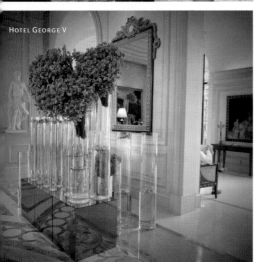

HOTEL GEORGE V

CHAMPS ELYSEES

ARC DE TRIOMPHE
DE CAROUSEL

JARDIN DES CHAMPS ELYSEES

Belle Époque design and also built for the exhibition of 1900. This building echoes the design of Invalides, which is across the Seine. The museum displays fine arts from antiquity to 1925 and also hosts short-term exhibits. Go inside to marvel at swirls of marble and garland-adorned moldings, and to take a break at the courtyard café, which is free to visit.

Outside, before crossing to the bridge, note the appropriately larger-than-life (10-feet) **statue of Winston Churchill**, unveiled in 1998 by Queen Elizabeth II. **Pont Alexandre** is another vestige of the exhibition of 1900, dedicated to France's friendship with Russia. The elegant arch of more than 300 feet is known for its gilded statuary—and for fashion photo shoots.

DOUBLE BACK ON PONT ALEXANDRE. GO RIGHT DOWN STAIRS AND WALK THE QUAY TO THE NEXT BRIDGE, PONT DE LA CONCORDE. GO UP, CROSS THE BUSY STREET, AND TAKE THE STAIRS TO THE RIGHT TO JARDIN DES TUILERIES. (PLACE DE LA CONCORDE IS VISITED IN WALKING TOUR FOUR.)

On the right as you top the stairs is **Musee de l'Orangerie**, built in 1852 as a place to grow citrus for the royals and now a treasure trove of Impressionist paintings. Step inside. Lines normally are short and the museum is not huge. The big payoff is the "Sistine Chapel of Impressionism," Claude Monet's Nympheas (Water Lilies). The paintings, basking in natural light from a sky-lit ceiling (thanks to a 2006 renovation), run the circumference of two, 40-foot-oval rooms, seamlessly converging 300 six-foot-tall paintings that Monet labored to complete during the last 30 years of his life. He died at age 86 in 1926. Taking in myriad hues and views of the ponds at his country home, the paintings evoke being in an aquarium. L'Orangerie

also displays a large sampling of works by Gauguin, Renoir, Cezanne, Matisse, Utrillo, Sisely, and others.

Across the way from l'Orangerie at the head of the gardens is another museum, **Jeu de Paume**. The former royal tennis courts became a museum in 1987, devoted to contemporary art that includes image techniques ranging from photographs to video.

Jardin des Tuileries was first laid out by Queen Catherine de Medici in 1564 and took its essential French-formal-garden design a century later, thanks to Louis XIV's landscape architect Andre le Notre (who also designed Versailles). Since opening to the public in 1667, the park has been where Parisians take refuge in the city. These days people lounge in comfortable chairs around the **Octagonal Pond** or stroll the wide, white-sand pathway lined by leafy trees. It's tempting to head straight down the great axis to the Louvre, but you might want to swerve broadly to take in side gardens, fountains, and sculptures. To appreciate the Tuileries, stop for an espresso or ice cream at one of the outdoor cafes. At the other end of the two-third-mile garden is the **Round Pond**, where children sail small boats.

Arc de Triomphe de Carousel is now the gateway to the Louvre. Like its larger version up the Champs Elysees, it was built on order of Napoleon after victories in Germany in 1806. Originally, the top was graced by a gilded chariot group looted from St. Mark's in Venice, but these works were returned in 1815.

A history of today's **Musee du Louvre** takes in much of the history of Paris. The former royal palace took shape over nearly 700 years, beginning with Philip II in the early

I. M. PEI PYRAMID, LOUVRE

12C and continued under the direction of 16 other sovereigns, emperors, and kings. It's safe to say none of them could imagine the sleek, 70-foot-high **glass pyramid designed by I. M. Pei** that has marked the entrance since 1989.

An original palace with towering walls on the western edge of Paris was once at this site. A museum since 1793, the Louvre holds some 35,000 artworks in numerous pavilions covering 652,000 square feet. Works cover Western art from the Middle Ages through 1848, and include significant offerings from ancient Greece, Rome, and Egypt. Though nowhere near the world's largest museum, it is the world's most visited. Unless you want to jet in to see the *Mona Lisa*, *Venus de Milo*, and *Winged Victory* on the run, you should plan a full day or three for a visit. But you can take a quick (free) look inside to fully appreciate Pei's vision. Rather than waiting in line at the pyramid, use the entrance to the left just beyond the stone archway of the Richelieu Pavilion. You'll get a peek at some of the antiquities on the way there, visible through a glass exterior. Steps lead down to the vast subterranean foyer of the Louvre, usually teaming with tourists and abuzz with a mélange of languages. Wide corridors lead to the museum's pavilions, each with several levels. For a comprehensive preview of the collections visit www.louvre.fr/en.

Hop on the central escalator for a ride up to the base of the pyramid, outside of which are reflecting pools and three dwarf pyramids. From this inside-out perspective you can see how this strikingly modern architecture compliments the three historic wings of the Palais du Louvre that enclose the Cour Napoleon.

END AT PALAIS ROYALE-MUSEE DU LOUVRE METRO STOP, LINE 1. IT'S ON RUE DE RIVOLI, AS YOU EXIT THE RICHELIEU PAVILION.

Louvre Entrance

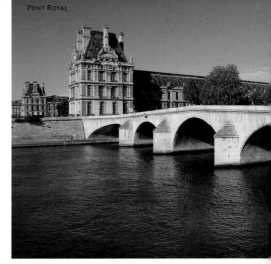

Pont Royal

Palais Royal-Louvre Museum Station

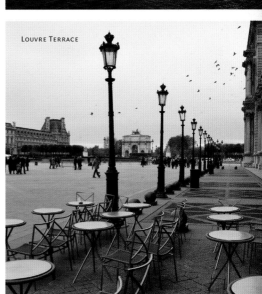

Louvre Terrace

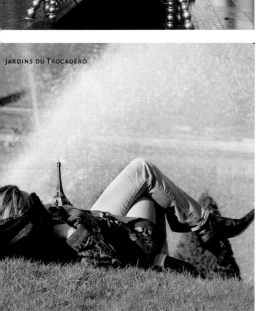

Jardins du Trocadero

Tuileries

QUAI AUGUSTIN

WALKING TOUR TWO

POSTCARDS:

Ile St. Louis ... Notre Dame ... Ile de la Cite ... Sainte Chapelle ... La Conciergerie ...
Left Bank ... Latin Quarter ... St. Etienne du Mont ... Pantheon ... Place de la
Contrescarpe ... Rue Mouffetard ... Arenes de Lutece ... Jardin des Plantes

THUMBNAIL:

The two islands in the Seine are the literal center of Paris—many would say at the
wellspring of modern Western culture. Armies from all of Europe crisscrossed this spot for
twenty centuries. On the Left Bank are narrow cobblestone streets and exotic shops that
captivate visitors. Streets wind up to the Pantheon, a route of the Romans and an environ
for writers ranging from Descartes to Dante to Hemingway. The walk ends at huge Jardin
des Plantes, with its formal gardens and museums that have catalogued the earth's natural
history for centuries.

BIG PICTURE:

Though doable at a leisurely pace, Walking Tour Two can easily be divided into two days,
with one day being the islands in the Seine, and the next a walk into the outer reaches of
the Latin Quarter, with a longer stay at Jardin de Plantes. Combined, you will see many of
the places for which Paris is famous, but this tour shows its more intimate, vintage spaces,
rather than the monumental expanses of Walking Tour One.

DISTANCE: 4.5 to 5 miles   TIME: 4.5 to 8.5 hours

Mouffetard Marché

POMI HALLES MOUFFETARD

POMI HALLES MOUFFETARD

RUE DE L'ARBALÈTE

St. Etienne Du Mont

Quai de Bourbon

Jardin Des Plantes

Notre Dame from Institut De Monde Arab

INSTITUT DE MONDE ARABE

CONCERGERIE

TOP OF PANTHEON

LES BOUQUINISTES

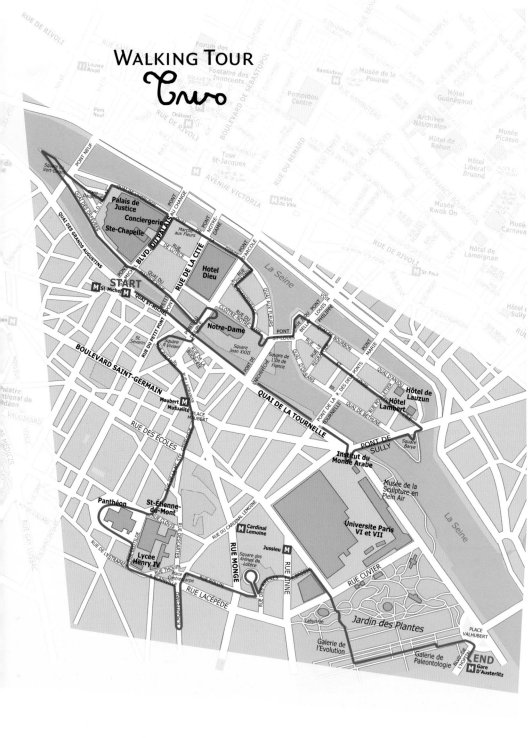

START AT ST. MICHEL-NORTE DAME STOP, RER, LINE C. (THE RER IS A TRAIN SYSTEM THAT CONNECTS INSIDE PARIS WITH THE METRO AND HONORS METRO TICKETS.)

FROM THE METRO EXIT, FACE THE SEINE AT THE BRIDGE NEAREST NOTRE DAME (PONT AU DOUBLE). DO NOT CROSS THE RIVER, BUT INSTEAD CROSS THE STREET AND GO DOWN THE STAIRS ALONG THE QUAY OF PORT DE LA TOURNELLE. CONTINUE UNDER TWO BRIDGES, AND WALK UP A RAMP TO STREET LEVEL AT THE THIRD BRIDGE, PONT DE SULLY.

You'll receive grand, broadside views of Notre Dame (visited later in this walk before leaving the islands) while walking along a broad quay. To get a bird's-eye preview of this walk, cross the street at Pont de Sully to the **Institut de Monde Arabe**. Entry is via a rear courtyard, and admission is free. Inside, take a glass elevator up through the open superstructure. The place is a cube of light. An outdoor terrace on the ninth floor is ideal for surveying the islands. A museum on the seventh floor has offerings from 20-plus Arab countries, with exhibits dating from third century BC Carthage.

CROSS PONT DU SULLY TO ILE ST. LOUIS. GO LEFT ALONG RUE ST. LOUIS EN L'ISLE— OCCASIONALLY LEAVING THIS INTIMATE CENTRAL STREET FOR SIGHTS ALONG THE QUAYS.

Ile St. Louis is named for Louis IX, the only French king ever to be made a saint, but it was not developed until the 17C, some 400 years after his death. The wealthy were able to construct quays and achieve the high ground worthy of lavish homes and quaint streets. To your right as you reach the island is a greenspace with a pleasant quay, **Parc Antoine Barye**, which is a vestige of the terraced gardens of Hotel de Bretonvilliers. An arch remaining from that building spans Rue Bretonvilliers. To the right at 2 Rue St. Louis is **Hotel Lambert**, built in 1640 for one of the developers, and a century later where Voltaire lived with his mistress. Along the northern quay (go right on Rue Poulletier and right again) is **Hotel de Lauzon**, the Hashish Club of the mid-1800s frequented by Balzac, Charles Baudelaire, Theophile Gautier, Delacroix, and other artists of the time. The hotel now hosts official receptions, none more prestigious the one in 1957 for Queen Elizabeth. The **church St. Louis en l'Isle**, built in 1640 on the main street but entered via steps on Rue Poulletier, is noted for its marble-and-gold spire, east-facing stained glass—and for a commemoration by the Pope in 1804.

Several of France's most famous women have been island residents. **Marie Curie** lived at 36 Quai Bethune, near Pont de la Tournelle. Sculptor **Camille Claudel**, Rodin's gifted student, lived on the other side of the island, at 19 Quai de Bourbon. A tormented genius, Claudel was moved to a mental hospital in 1913 to live her remaining 30 years. To see Claudel's place, go right near the end of the street on **Rue le Regrattier**. At the corner nearest the quay you'll see the bas-relief of **Femme Sans Tete**, a notorious woman—coveted and beautiful—who was decapitated after a lover's quarrel in the late 16C. At #6 on this street is where the poet Baudelaire kept another notorious woman, his tempestuous mistress, the exotic Creole actress/dancer **Jeanne Duval**. Dubbed "Venus Noire," she was precursor in many ways to Josephine Baker, who shook the club scene 80 years later.

In addition to being a gateway to the homes of the rich-and-talented departed, Ile St. Louis is also a great place to pick up a baked treat from a patisserie. Or try an ice cream at one of several Berthillon stores, including its headquarters at #31. For a respite on the river, head to **Quai de Bourbon** at the very tip of the island.

AT THE FAR END OF ILE ST. LOUIS, CROSS PONT ST. LOUIS ONTO ILE DE LA CITE.

The current **Pont St. Louis** is the ninth bridge to connect the two disparate island worlds. The first collapsed on opening day in 1643, drowning 20. The existing span normally drowns visitors with street music that enlivens the entrance to **Square Jean XXIII**, the park at the restful backside of Notre Dame. Continue along the square on Rue de Cloitre Notre Dame to visit the **Museum de Notre Dame**, crammed with artifacts. Then double back.

FROM RUE DE CLOITRE NOTRE DAME, VEER RIGHT ON RUE CHANOINESSE. THEN GO RIGHT ON RUE DE LA COLOMBE AND LEFT ALONG QUAI DE LA CORSE.

At #24 on curving Rue Chanoinesse is an oft-photographed and highly reviewed café, **Aux Vieux Paris d'Arcole**, set in a building that dates from 1512. Then, after a walk along the quay that passes two bridges, you'll come to a burst of fragrance and color that is the **Marche aux Fleurs** in **Place Louis Lepine**. Sunday is a day to tweet, when live birds add to the show.

The center of Ile de la Cite (jog left on Boulevard du Palais) is taken up by the **Palais du Justice**, most of which is occupied by working buildings for the courts and police, and not intended for tourists. Closest to the river is **La Conciergerie**, known most as the dungeon fortress that housed 3,000 prisoners before they met the guillotine elsewhere in the city during late 1700s French Revolution.

Among the condemned were mastermind Robespierre and Queen Marie Antoinette, whose cell was later converted to a small chapel in her honor. The building is on the site of the early Roman governors' headquarters (the island was city's most defensible real estate in those days). The site was then the palace for French monarchs until they moved to the Louvre in the late 14C. La Conciergerie turned from prison to National Monument in 1914.

Next door (look for the line of people) is **Sainte Chapelle**, built over seven years, beginning in 1246, to house some of the booty from the Crusades, including the Crown of Thorns and fragments of the True Cross. Visitors these days cram in to see what is still state-of-the-art stained glass—15 towering windows, narrowly separated and streaming bejeweled light in primarily blue and red hues. Time may not permit a visit during this complete walking tour.

CONTINUE ALONG THE QUAY, GO LEFT AT RUE DE HARLAY, RIGHT THROUGH PLACE DAUPHINE, AND CONTINUE TO THE TIP OF THE ISLAND AT SQUARE DU VERT GALANT.

Understated **Place Dauphine** dates from 1860 and was named for Henry IV's son, who became Louis XII. Untouched by Haussmann's 19C revamp of the island, the benches amid chestnut trees have long been contemplative places for socialites, including actors Yves Montand and Simone Signoret, who lived in the residences overlooking Place Dauphine.

Set at the natural level of the island before it was built up in 1570, **Square Vert Galant** is a meeting place for lovers, owning to the romantic setting at its green tip. It was a spot favored by the island's namesake,

Marché aux Fleurs

Place Dauphine

Femme Sans Tête

Pont Neuf

beloved Henry IV, who fathered children by more than one mistress and was known as the Merry Monarch and the "gay old dog." A statue of the king presides over the upper terrace of the square.

FROM SQUARE GALANT, DOUBLE BACK, EITHER ALONG THE QUAY OR STREET, TO NOTRE DAME.

Pont Neuf, closest to the island's tip, is the oldest surviving bridge, dating from 1607. Earlier bridges here were the last line of defense for rulers clinging onto the island from the time of the original Roman settlement (called Lutece or Lutecia) and extending through the Middle Ages. Across the river is **Quai des Grands Augustins**, which was the first on the river, built in 1313 around a monastery at that site. The quay provided high ground for buildings.

A history of **Notre Dame** would have to begin with the tribe of boatmen of Celtic origins, Parisii, who lived here for several centuries—a society advanced enough to mint gold coins. After prolonged battles, the Parisii lost a final battle to Julius Caesar and the Romans in 52 BC. Although Gallo-Roman temples to Jupiter were erected in the fourth and sixth centuries, the first stone version of this cathedral was not laid until 1163 (by Pope Alexander III) and took well over a century to complete. Dozens of architects have added touches over the ensuing six centuries—including in the 13C when flying buttresses were added to further open the interior. During the Revolution it was pillaged and renamed the Temple of Reason. Crown jewels were looted and 28 ancient statues of the Kings of Judea, mistaken for historical French kings, were destroyed.

The cathedral of **Notre Dame** faced a real threat not long after its crowning glory in 1804: At the cathedral, a victorious Napoleon was made emperor by Pope Pius the VII—or rather the immodest general took the crown and placed it on his own head. In subsequent years the emperor hatched plans to demolish the church and start afresh. After years of debate, the edifice was saved, largely due to the popularity of Victor Hugo's 1831 novel, the *Hunchback of Notre Dame*. Hugo called its architectural discord a "symphony of stone." During a 20-plus-year period in the 19C, the cathedral took the integrated Gothic-Romanesque form of Louis XIV's genius architect, Eugene Viollet le Duc. Among his touches were the 300-foot steeple, floral motifs, and the three portals along the west (front) façade.

Entry, which is free but involves a line in peak periods, is via the right-side portal. The grandness and detail inside can be overwhelming. Don't forget to focus on the rose windows in the north transept, some 70 feet in diameter. And look for another stained glass window from 1769, a 40-foot high depiction of Christ with saints, apostles, and angels.

The large plaza in front the church, **Place du Parvis Notre Dame**, is a good place to hear the 13-ton bell ring from the south tower belfry. To climb from the plaza to the belfry—230 feet high among the gargoyles—head for the north tower. A narrow spiral staircase of more than 400 worn stone steps (claustrophobics beware) reaches the open spaces of both towers. An admission is charged. (You may not have time, if doing the whole walking tour.) Prior to 1865, the parvis was a warren of winding alleyways, more densely packed than the Left Bank. But Baron Haussmann's citywide redo opened the space on behalf of Napoleon III.

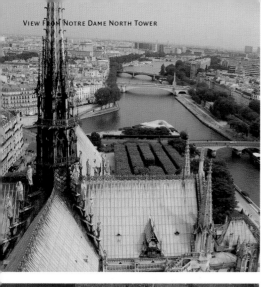

VIEW FROM NOTRE DAME NORTH TOWER

NOTRE DAME

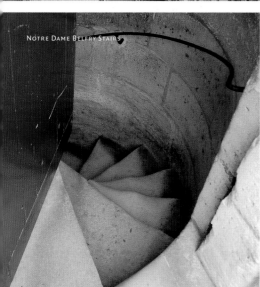

NOTRE DAME BELFRY STAIRS

POINT ZERO

NOTRE DAME

SQUARE RENÉ VIVIANI

Just about everyone will want to stand at **Point Zero**, marked by a bronze star about 100 feet in front of the west portal. The star is from 1769, but it marks the spot from which all distances in France have been measured for centuries. To the right on the parvis, as if emerging from medieval hoarfrost, is a **Statue of Charlemagne**, King of the Franks until 814 AD. Charlemagne's victories over the Muslims unified the post-Roman nation that would be modern France. Finally, in the section of the parvis closest to the street is the below-ground (more than 200 feet) **Crypte Archeologique**. It holds foundations and vestiges of buildings that date from the third-century city of Lutetia, which were discovered and preserved during the construction of a modern-day parking lot.

CROSS PONT AU DOUBLE TO THE LEFT BANK. ON YOUR RIGHT, ENTER SQUARE RENE VIVIANI.

Small **Square Rene Viviani**, the site of student dorms 800 years ago, is the loveliest park on the Seine, and decorated with elements from Notre Dame. At the back of the park, behind a 400-year-old, tired-looking acacia tree, is **St. Julien le Pauvre**, one of Paris' three oldest churches, completed in 1230 after fifty years of labor by monks. During the Middle Ages, St. Julien le Pauvre was a stopover for the Pilgrimage to Santiago de Compostela in Spain. The intimate church today is a venue for concerts. With roots even older is **St. Severin**, the back entrance of which is just across Rue du Petit Pont. Check out the interior, with its double ambulatory, forest of columns leading to vaults, and brilliant stained glass. Severin was a 6C hermit, known for his kindness, who was later proclaimed a saint by St. Cloud, the grandson of King Clovis. The Flamboyant Gothic church was

erected in the 13C, but was rebuilt in 1452 after a fire and drastically altered in the 17C. Before the Seine was tamed by quays, these church sites were on the dry ground nearest the river.

BEHIND ST. JULIEN DE PAUVRE, WALK LEFT ON RUE GALANDE. VEER RIGHT AT RUE LAGRANGE TO PLACE MAUBERT.

The corner of **Rue Galande**, one of the oldest streets in Paris, marks the start of the ancient route to Rome. At #42 is a 14C bas-relief of St. Julien helping Christ across the Seine, the oldest "street sign" in the city. Galande merges with **Rue Lagrange**, which in the Middle Ages was a thriving den of students and site of populist uprisings. Among the rabble rousers was **Dante Alighieri**, who drew inspiration to write The Divine Comedy. The action spilled to **Place Maubert**, which became a crime ridden skid row. Now it's a desirable neighborhood, site of outdoor markets (Tuesday, Thursday, Saturday) and setting for Diane Johnson's breezy novel-made-movie, Le Divorce.

CROSS TO THE RIGHT SIDE OF THE PLACE MAUBERT AND CONTINUE UPHILL ON SMALLER RUE DE LA MONTAGNE STE. GENEVIEVE. VEER RIGHT AT A SMALL PLACE AND CONTINUE TO THE PANTHEON.

The village street curves uphill and passes a small place, enclave to students, before reaching (on your left) **St. Etienne du Mont**. One of Paris' finest Gothic churches, it began in 1492—on the site of a 6C abbey built by King Clovis. Henry IV consecrated the church in 1626, although the bell tower and west façade date from the Renaissance. Inside is a shrine to **St. Genevieve** (422-512), favored by King Clovis, whose prayers and advice are said to have diverted the invading army of Attila

Rue Galande

Pantheon

Rue de la Montagne St. Genevieve

the Hun from his march on Paris. She is the beautiful patron saint whose name is still invoked when the city is in trouble. The interior of St. Etienne du Mont is noted for luminous tall aisles, the golden stone of the nave, and double-staircase with wood-carved rood (crucifix on a screen). The staircase dates from 1541 and is one of the few from that era remaining in Paris.

The **Pantheon** is lofted on the hill, at a strategic site of a former Gallo-Roman fortress of the colony of Lutetia. This Roman replica was built by Louis XV in 1764. He had called upon Sainte Genevieve when he was ill and vowed to build a shrine to her if he recovered. The Neo-classical church took 26 years to build, completed in the year of the Revolution when monastic orders were abolished—and it became a "temple to the nation." Despite a lack of windows, the vast interior glows. From April to October, the price of admission includes a chance to climb several spiral staircases to high interior balconies and a walkway outside around the dome—one of the best views of Paris. You'll want to see the murals of Joan of Arc and to stare at the recreation of Foucault's Pendulum, the 1851 experiment that proved the earth's rotation. And don't miss the sprawling mausoleum in the basement, where you'll find the crypts of Voltaire, Alexandre Dumas, Victor Hugo, Emile Zola, Rousseau, and other French greats.

CONTINUE AROUND THE FRONT OF THE PANTHEON TO RUE CLOTILDE, WHICH RUNS ALONG ITS BACK. GO RIGHT AND THEN GO LEFT ON RUE DE L'ESTRAPADE. THEN VEER RIGHT ON RUE BLAINVILLE AND CONTINUE DOWN TO PLACE DE LA CONTRESCARPE.

On the left at Rue Clotilde is the Lycee Henry IV, where Jean Paul Sartre had his day job as a professor. If you walk a block

PLACE DE LA CONTRESCARPE

farther left to Rue Clovis you can see what's left of the 6C basilica, the Tour de Clovis, and also a remaining section of the Philippe Auguste Wall, which enclosed Paris at the turn of the 13C.

Narrow Rue Blainville ends at **Place de la Contrescarpe**, where the voices of trendsetters of the Latin Quarter murmur from several pricey cafes (Café Delmas is a good choice). Trees adorn a small central *place*. Historically the neighborhood was known for its squalor. Samuel Beckett's lonely characters in *Waiting for Godot* drank their wine here. Hemingway, who wrote *A Moveable Feast* here, was inspired by "the smell of dirty sweat and poverty and drunkenness." His favorite spot was Café de Amateurs on Mouffetard, which he called "a cesspool."

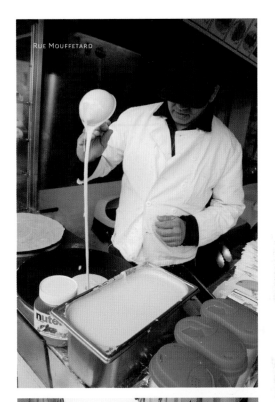

RUE MOUFFETARD

GO RIGHT IN THE PLACE TO RUE MOUFFETARD, WALK DOWN AS FAR AS YOU LIKE, AND THEN DOUBLE BACK.

Rue Mouffetard was the beginning of the ancient route leaving Lutetia for Rome. Crepe stands, pubs, Greek restaurants, pastry shops, and a market at the bottom make this one of the city's best walking streets. Near the market, at #3 Rue de l'Arbalete, is where Auguste Rodin was born in 1840. Higher up, at #60 is the **Pot de Fer Fountain**, of Italianate design that was commissioned by Marie de Medici to send water to the Luxembourg Palace.

LEAVE PLACE DE LA CONTRESCARPE ON RUE DU CARDINAL LEMOINE, STRAIGHT ACROSS FROM MOUFFETARD. GO RIGHT IMMEDIATELY ON RUE ROLLIN. CONTINUE DOWN THE NARROW RUE AND ITS STEPS, AND GO LEFT ON RUE DES ARENES.

Down Lemoine, at #74, is the first Paris home in 1922 for **Ernest and Hadley**

RUE ROLLIN

Hemingway; he and his fist wife had to go up five flights of stairs. But the writer-on-the-block award might go to **James Joyce**, who completed *Ulysses* at #71. On the other hand, both might give the nod to philosopher **Rene Descartes**, who in the early 1600s lived nearby at #14 Rue Rollin.

As Rue Arenes descends on a curve, walk left into the center of a neighborhood park. From there you might guess that **Arenes de Lutece** is a first-century arena where crowds of 15,000 would watch gladiators do battle among themselves and with wild beasts. The arena had been urban legend until discovered during the excavation of a building in 1869. It was fully unearthed by 1918. About half the stones are originals in this partial reconstruction.

LEAVE THE ARENA AND CROSS BUSY RUE LINNE. JOG RIGHT AND THEN GO LEFT ON RUE GUY DE LA BROSSE. THEN GO RIGHT ON RUE JUSSIEU AND CONTINUE ACROSS RUE CUVIER INTO JARDIN DES PLANTES AT A GATE FOR THE RESTAURANT AT ADDRESS #47. (A MAIN GATE FOR THE GARDEN IS UP CUVIER TO YOUR RIGHT, AT THE CORNER WITH RUE LINNE.)

Within the 70 acres of **Jardin des Plantes** are excellent museums, a zoo, and several gardens—a day's worth of exploring that you will probably only have time to walk through. Louis XIII asked his physician, Guy de la Brosse, to found a garden to study medicinal herbs and plants. It became the first public garden in Paris in 1640, but was expanded significantly in 1739 by Comte de Buffon. Though a major tourist attraction, the gardens are a university campus, focused on research and education.

From the restaurant entrance, go across the park, passing greenhouses— large mid-19C glass-and-wrought iron conservatories. Up to the right is the **Labyrinth**, a spiral walk through a hedge to a hill with historical significance but no real view. Boardering one side of the gardens are the four museums that comprise **Musee d'Historie Naturelle**. At the upper end is its big-splash attraction, the **Grande Galerie de l'Evolution**. The interior features a Noah's Ark-like procession led by bull elephants down the middle of an open, five-story hall with open walkways. The lighting is subdued and spectacular throughout. Exhibits trace virtually all animal life since the earth's origins. The poor dodo bird has a glass case all alone. Opened in 1899, the gallery was renovated extensively in 1994.

Choose one of the broad sandy paths past the statue of Buffon through the formal center of **Jardin de Plantes**. Lime, olive, and chestnut trees shade lawns, benches, and statuary. **The Rose Garden** features several hundred species. The fairly small **Menagerie** (zoo) is to the left at the other end— look for the circular La Rotonde. On the right is perhaps the garden's real treasure, the **Galerie de Paleontologie et Anatomie Comparee**. Inside are several thousands of animal skeletons—land, sea, and air—meticulously assembled frames and grinning skulls of all sizes. The specimens are from the 1700s and 1800s, most all bearing their original labels. Set in the historic building, the gallery preserves the scientific methodology of the time, as well as the creatures gathered from throughout the world. The library at Jardin des Plantes contains treasured botanical and biological manuscripts.

END AT GARE D'AUSTERLITZ STOP ON RER, LINE C. AT THE BOTTOM END OF JARDIN DES PLANTES, GO RIGHT ACROSS BUSY BLVD. DE HOPITAL TO THE STATION.

WALKING TOUR THREE

POSTCARDS:

Left Bank ... Place St. Michel ... Latin Quarter ... Musee de Moyen Age ... Sorbonne ... St. Sulpice ... Jardin du Luxembourg ... Rue du Cherche Midi ... St. Germain des Pres ... Musee Delacroix ... Musee d'Orsay

THUMBNAIL:

The exotic cobblestone alleys of the Latin Quarter wind toward the university student's enclave and the site of Roman ruins, which currently archive some of Paris's oldest treasures. Open-air market streets lead to the ancient church of St. Suplice and then onto Luxembourg Gardens, where Parisians relax in plenty of space. The route swings back toward the Seine, through the literary cafés (Hemingway, Sartre, et al) of St. Germain des Pres, then take in a series of narrow streets sprinkled with galleries, boutiques, antiques, and famous restaurants. The walk concludes along the quay to Musee D'Orsay, the former railway station that is now, to some, the city's premier museum.

BIG PICTURE:

Walking Tour Three is kissing cousin to the previous walk—more of the Latin Quarter to take in other better known sights of Paris. While Tour Three includes some of the most ancient (pre-Roman) artifacts, the walk is more about the "now" of Paris than the past—boulevard life, campus atmosphere, places where locals relax, and cafes frequented by the glitterati from around the world. You'll probably wind up taking fewer lengthy stopovers and spend more time ambling, fueled by sidewalk stimulation.

DISTANCE: 4.5 to 5.5 miles   TIME: 4 to 6 hours

QUAI VOLTAIRE

BOULEVARD ST. GERMAIN

LES DEUX MAGO

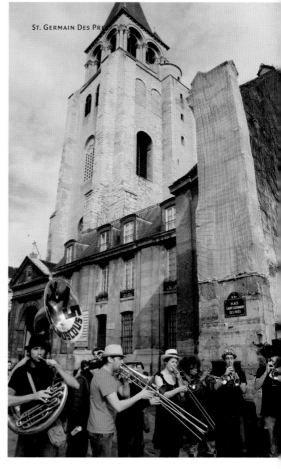

ST. GERMAIN DES PRE

LATIN QUARTER

RUE DU CHAT QUI PECHE

BAR
RESTAURANT

RUE DU CHERCHE-MIDI

Poilâne

ST. SUPLICE

MUSÉE DU MOYEN ÂGE

RUE DE LA HUCHETTE

JARDIN DU LUXEMBOURG CAFÉ

WALKING TOUR
Three

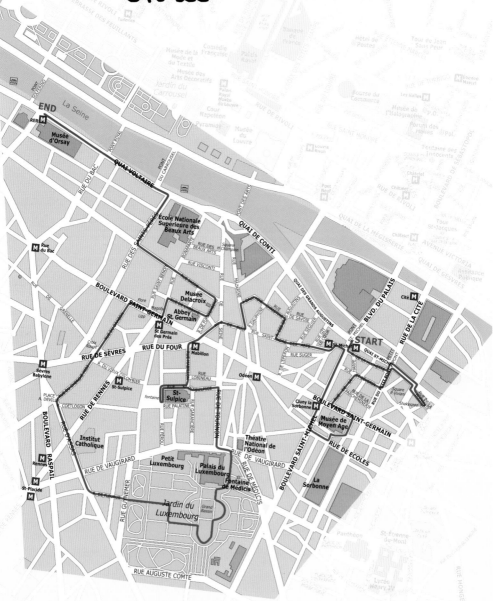

START AT ST. MICHEL METRO STOP, LINE 4.

FACING AWAY FROM THE RIVER, WALK TO LARGE PLACE ST. MICHEL. GO LEFT ON RUE DE LA HUCHETTE. AT RUE DU PETIT PONT, JOG LEFT. THEN GO RIGHT ON RUE DE LA BUCHERIE.

At #27 Quai St. Michael is the residence of **Henri Matisse** in 1905, when you could live here and still be poor; the painter attracted Gertrude Stein's patronage before she moved on to Picasso. The cobblestones of narrow **Rue de la Huchette** are magnets for tourists. The daily buzz of commerce is followed by nightlife at clubs like Caveau de la Huchette, at address #5. The 16C building with many historical threads has been wowing jazz lovers since 1946, hosting performances by the greats, including Count Basie. A young Napoleon, not known as a party animal, lived at #10 in 1795. Amid the local color, you might walk right by the narrowest street in Paris, a dreary alley, **Rue du Chat qui Peche**. When crossing **Rue Petit Pont**, look left to see the bridge at the site of the first across the river (though this stone version dates from the 18C). The bridge marked the start of the original route out of Paris. **Rue de la Bucherie** in the Middle Ages was at the high-water mark of the Seine and was the site of loading docks for logs. Today the street is best known for **Shakespeare & Company**, an English language bookstore at #37. (This store opened in 1964; Sylvia Beach's original writer's hangout between the world wars was near Place Odeon, at #8 Rue Dupuytren.)

DOUBLE BACK ON BUCHERIE TO RUE PETIT PONT AND GO LEFT. THEN GO RIGHT ON RUE ST. SEVERIN AND LEFT ON RUE DE LA HARPE. CONTINUE TO AND CROSS BLVD. ST. GERMAIN.

The narrowest house in Paris, 8-feet wide, is at #22 Rue St. Severin. **Rue Harpe**, a major thoroughfare before being segmented by Haussmann's redevelopment, is now home to student housing and a grab bag of affordable ethnic eateries—North African, Greek, Chinese, Vietnamese, and Turkish. You'll cross **Rue de Parcheminerie**, where paper was produced and books printed in the 16C, and today is the site of the Abbey Bookshop, another refuge English readers.

Across Blvd. St. Germain is the backside of **Musee Nationale de Moyen Age** (formerly Musee Cluny), which also includes Roman baths, **Palais des Thermes**. The museum is repository of art and artifacts from the Middle Ages. Walk left through gardens to the courtyard in front. You'll have time for a visit (an admission is charged). Hotel Cluny is one of only two remaining examples of medieval architecture in Paris, built first by abbots in 1310 and rebuilt extensively as a private residence in 1510. These structures rest in part on the five-foot-thick walls of the Roman baths that date from the second century. Inside, filtered light wafts from the 50-foot-high vaulted ceilings into the **Frigidarium**, the last of three phases of Roman body care that began with the hot Caldarium. The museum's collection includes a few of the 21 heads of the Kings of Judea Gallery recovered from Notre Dame, as well as tons of ceramics, sculpted gold and silver, and everyday objects of the Middle Ages. Exhibits are displayed along an exhaustive tour of the building's stairways, cubbyholes, and anterooms. Getting the most attention, considered to be the greatest art from the Middle Ages, is a series of six wool-and-silk tapestries, collectively named **The Lady and the Unicorn** (La Dame a la Licorne). Though the subject of much interpretation, the dark, lyrical tapestries depict a noblewoman with a lion and unicorn in various settings, and are widely thought to represent the five senses, with the sixth tapestry being a portrayal of love and understanding. This building with a long past became a museum in 1945.

Across Rue de Ecoles (angle past the restful park of **Place Paul Painleve**) is the **Sorbonne**, the 13C college to which the Latin Quarter owes its intellectual heritage and name (Latin was the language common to world scholars up until recent centuries). The school's roots can be traced from philosopher Pierre Abelard, who was ousted from Notre Dame for challenging monastic discipline, after which he attracted a student following. More scholars arrived in 1469, when France's first printing press was set up here. Though tourists aren't free to wander, you can catch of glimpse of the domed church that dates from 1635, the oldest existing building on campus. Many of today's literati hang out nearby at **Brasserie Balazar** (#49 Rue de Ecoles), as described by New Yorker writer Adam Gopnik in his recent memoir, *Paris to the Moon*. Journalists have gabbed here since the 1920s, when James Thurber set the tone.

CROSS BLVD. ST. MICHEL AND GO RIGHT TO PLACE ST. MICHEL. GO LEFT TO ADJOINING PLACE ST. ANDRE DES ARTS. LEAVE THE PLACE BY VEERING RIGHT ONTO RUE ST. ANDRE DES ARTS. CONTINUE TO RUE DES GRANDS AUGUSTINS AND GO RIGHT, AND THEN IMMEDIATELY LEFT ON RUE CHRISTINE.

The imposing **Fontaine St. Michael**, designed by Davioud, depicts the Archangel Michael flinging the devil into the water. The fountain was situated to the side of the place in 1860, rather than at its center, in order to cover the end view of the adjacent street. The **Allard** bistro at #41 Rue St. Andre des Arts is known for its seafood and frog legs, but also for the legs of **Brigitte Bardot,** who loved the place. For stylish 17C and 18C architecture, look for addresses #27, #28, and #52.

When **Pablo Picasso** had money in 1936, he resided at #7 Rue des Grands Augustins. Not far away, at #5 on the posh, sedate **Rue Christine** lived his patron, **Gertrude Stein**, with her lover **Alice B. Toklas**. (Stein bought an early work for 30 bucks and said Picasso was one of the world's three geniuses, the others being Alfred North Whitehead and herself.) Stein's extensive Impressionist collection hung at this residence, which was originally the digs of Queen Christine of Sweden. Stein died in 1946; Toklas lived here until 1964 when she was forced to move, three years before her death.

CROSS RUE DAUPHINE AND ENTER PASSAGE DAUPHINE. COME OUT TO RUE MAZARINE, AND GO LEFT. THEN TAKE THE NEXT RIGHT AT CARREFOUR DE BUCI TO RUE DE BUCI.

The quiet escape of Place Dauphine opens to a more lively and storied **Rue Mazarine**. France's greatest playwright, **Moliere** (1622-1673), first brought his comedic skills to the stage at #12, and then formed his first acting company at #42—the beginning in essence of what later became Comedie Francaise. At #13 is the oldest café in Paris (1686) **Café Procope**, which was a forum for news and gossip during and before the Revolution. Among the voices were those of Danton, Rousseau, Voltaire, Robesperiere, and Benjamin Franklin. **Oscar Wilde** held court at Procope about a century later, in 1890, while the Irish playwright completed a work in French. Rue Mazarine is known for numerous fine restaurants.

You'll enter a lively marketplace and street scene after turning right at **Carrefour de**

St. Andre Des Artes

Saint Severin

Fontaine St. Michel

Rue de la Bucherie

Buci, where you can also see a section of the Philippe Auguste wall that surrounded Paris in 1180. The nexus of commerce is at the corner with Rue de Seine, where the quarter's arty gentry shop, along with number of tourists, who attract the occasional huckster. Watch your wallet.

FOLLOW BUCI AND CROSS BUSY BLVD. ST. GERMAIN TO RUE DU FOUR. GO IMMEDIATELY LEFT ON RUE MABILLON AND CONTINUE TO RUE SAINT SULPICE.

The stone arcade of Rue Mabillon (now home to Le Gap) sets up a broadside view of the spectacular **Saint Sulpice**. The church was built with stops and starts over a century, beginning in 1646. Six architects have contributed varying styles. Refurbishment continues to this day. The imposing interior features six frescoes by Delacroix created while he listened to services in 1855. One of the world's largest organs (some 6,600 pipes) was emplaced in 1781 in the west nave—also the setting for a violent scene in the *Da Vinci Code* movie. Of most interest perhaps is the marble obelisk in the north transept. It is positioned so that sunrays deflect upon a copper band imbedded along a meridian line in the floor to mark the solstices and equinoxes. In the plaza in front, chestnut trees surround the **Fontaine des Quatres Eveques** (Four Bishops, 1844), who point in the four cardinal directions.

FACING THE FRONT ENTRANCE OF ST. SULPICE, GO ALONG THE LEFT SIDE (ON RUE ST. SULPICE), AND THEN TURN RIGHT ON RUE DE TOURNON. CONTINUE, CROSS BUSY RUE VAUGIRARD, AND JOG LEFT TO ENTER THE GATES FOR JARDIN DU LUXEMBOURG.

Elegant shops with 18C facades line wide **Rue de Tournon.** Your nose will appreciate **Au Nom de la Rose** at #4, where a rose is

PASSAGE DAUPHINE

not just a rose. Close by is **Bonpoint**, where you can spend a ton of money on kids' clothes and visit a courtyard café.

On your left past the garden gate is the 1863 **Fontaine Medicis**, a sublime Italianate grotto adorned with Pan and Diana love statues, posed under a leafy ceiling. Artist Salomon de Brosse created this space of artful solitude.

On nice days, **Jardin du Luxembourg** quietly absorbs legions of leisure-seekers, and has since Marie de Medici first laid it out in 1615. Its nearly 60 acres are adorned with a forest of leafy trees, some 80 statues, two fountains, tennis and boules courts, and the largest playground in Paris (French kids play loud and rough). The focus of this grand space is the **Grand Bassin**, a pond encircled by chairs, the surface of which normally floats a fleet of toy sailboats. **Palais du Luxembourg**, with its weighty Tuscan columns, lords over north end gardens. Designed by the queen in the style of the Pitti Palace of her native Florence, the building has housed the French Senate for two centuries. The palace became a Nazi headquarters during WWII.

FROM THE FOUNTAIN, CURVE RIGHT AROUND THE BALUSTRADE ABOVE THE POND AND CONTINUE THROUGH THE PARK TO EXIT ON WEST SIDE AT RUE DE FLEURUS.

The statues posed around the terraces beyond the balustrade are the **Dames de France**, a tribute to queens and illustrious women. The west side of the park is often lively, with the oldest carousel in Paris spinning alongside a puppet performance by **Theatre des Marionettes**. In the formal hedges near the park exit in **Jardin Anglais** is a Statue of Liberty, which is the original bronze model used by sculptor Frederic Bartholdi to make New York's version;

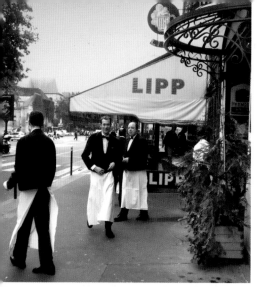

LIPP

ST. GERMAIN

Le Petit Zinc

RUE DES SAINTS PERES

JARDIN DU LUXEMBOURG

RUE BERNARD PALISSY

Le Rive Gauche

it was placed here in 1906. This swing through the gardens to the west gate follows the path taken by **Hemingway** after his divorce from Hadley in 1926, when, drunk and tearful, he pushed her possessions in a wheelbarrow to her new residence at 35 Rue de Fleurus. (With his second wife, Paris Vogue writer Pauline Pfeiffer, Hemingway moved close by, to #5 Rue Ferou, where he wrote *A Farewell to Arms*. Rue Ferou runs into Rue Vaugirard, west of the palace. Painter **Joan Miro**, a friend, worked at their residence occasionally.)

CONTINUE ON RUE FLEURUS, GO RIGHT ON RUE D'ASSAS, AND CONTINUE THREE LONG BLOCKS. TURN RIGHT ON RUE DE CHERCHE-MIDI. CONTINUE STRAIGHT ACROSS A PLACE TO RUE DRAGON.

The only French government plaque to commemorate an American is at **#27 Rue de Fleurus**, home of **Gertrude Stein** from 1903 to 1938. This where Matisse met Picasso, and artists from all walks considered themselves lucky to come and enjoy conversation and one of the hash brownies baked by Alice B. Toklas. One visitor was **F. Scott Fitzgerald** and his zany wife **Zelda**, who spent the summer of 1925 nearby. (To see their lavish rental with wrought-iron balconies, jog right from Rue d'Assas onto Rue Vaugirard to #25.)

On Rue d'Assas at the corner with Vaugirard is the **Institut Catholique de Paris**, founded in 1875, where theology students earn advanced degrees. On the university complex (on Vaugirard) is **St. Joseph des Carmes**, dating from 1613. This church is where 120 priests refused to avow the new order in 1792 during the Revolution and were massacred.

Vibrant **Rue Cherche-Midi** draws hip Parisians to its boutiques, quirky antique stores and small cafes. The biggest crowd is usually at **#8 Pain Polaine**, where crusty round loaves have been baked in a wood-fired oven since 1932. The bread is shipped throughout the world. The street ends at **Carrefour de la Croix Rouge**, the focal point of this fashion quarter that since 1988 has been noted for its statue *Centaur* by Cesar—an homage to Picasso who would appreciate its bizarre components. Fashion becomes slightly more upscale on **Rue du Dragon**, across the *place*. Overhead are the balconies of 17C homes. At #30 is **Victor Hugo's home** as a young man. Halfway down, take a detour right on photogenic Rue Bernard Palissy, where at #7 is **Les Editions de Minuit**, the publisher of **Samuel Beckett**.

AT WIDE BLVD. ST. GERMAIN, JOG RIGHT, THEN CROSS.

From Rue du Dragon you enter **Boulevard St. Germain**, traditionally the gathering spot for the intelligencia and trendsetters of the Left Bank—though today the boulevard is as much a tourist attraction, since designer fashion outlets have taken over some offices of publishers and agents. The scene centers around the holy triumvirate of cafes: Brasserie Lipp, Café de Flore, and Café de Deux Magots. To your right on this side of the boulevard is **Brasserie Lipp**, serving Alsatian foods like the cold potato salad and beer that Hemingway wrote about in *A Moveable Feast*. The in-crowd sits downstairs. Side-by-side across the boulevard are **Café de Flore** and **Café de Deux Magots**, rivals that historically have vied to be the most cool—though the two also have shared famous patrons. Flore in the 1940s was the birthplace of existentialism, where Sartre and Simone Beauvoir had a table and Camus frequently hung out (though he and Sartre did not get along). Deux Magots (Two Mandarins) was favored by Picasso and later the surrealist artists. In the 1950s writers like Gore Vidal and James Baldwin lent Deux Magots a new relevancy. These days, Flore may have the edge as the place to be, while Deux Magots caters to tourists—but these cerebral sands are always shifting. Some of the real elite probably imbibe more often on the street between the two, **Rue St. Benoit**, at places like Le Petit Zinc.

These century-old watering holes are new kids on the block compared to the **Abbey St. Germain des Pres**, source of the 6th arrondissement's cultural rootstock. The first basilica built here was in 542 A.D., under the reign of Frankish King Childebert I. It was pillaged during the Middle Ages, three times by the Vikings, and once by the Normans. The edifice was substantially rebuilt in 1163. The bell tower remains and is the city's oldest. By the late 18C, the power of the Benedictine Abbey reached an apex, with a domain that included lands and gardens that extended west to today's Champs de Mars. Turf wars with students from the Sorbonne—heralding the emergence of the university as an independent political institution—resulted in the deaths of dozens of students at the hands of the monks. Retribution came during the Revolution, when some 300 monks and priests were killed, and the church partially demolished. Much restoration was done in 1822. The cavernous interior swallows the light from stained glass windows. Descartes' tombstone is in one of the naves. The north wall is mostly from the 11C, a reminder of the church's origins.

FACING THE FRONT OF ST. GERMAIN DES PRES, JOG LEFT AND THEN TURN RIGHT ON RUE L'ABBAYE. AT RUE DE FURSTEMBERG, GO LEFT AND THEN LEFT AGAIN ON RUE JACOB.

Rue de l'Abbaye, formerly home to vintage bookstores, has attracted designer shops from the Right Bank. Turn left at the corner onto **Place Furstemberg** and you're in a period set piece—where director Martin Scorsese filmed the last scene of *Age of Innocence*. The courtyard is the address for the **Musee Delacroix**, which was the Romantic painter's home and workshop from 1857 until he died six years later. Eugene Delacroix's former studio overlooks a garden. An admission is charged.

The beauty of **Rue Jacob** is subdued, hidden in courtyards that lead to gardens and stone staircases of posh residences. An example is #14 is where composer **Richard Wagner** did much of his work. Chic hotels, like Marronniers at #21 and de Deux Continents at #25 (though perhaps past their primes) normally require bookings months in advance. At #56, formerly **Hotel d'York**, **Benjamin Franklin** in 1783 met with a representative of England's King George III to sign the document recognizing American independence. He lived at #52, which was also a residence for **Thomas Jefferson**. All this may not be as enticing as the macaroons at **Laduree**, on the corner at 21 Rue Bonaparte.

FROM JACOB, TURN RIGHT ON RUE DES SAINTS PERES. CONTINUE TO THE END AND GO LEFT ON QUAI VOLTAIRE. OPTION: CROSS THE BUSY STREET AND AT THE NEXT BRIDGE (PONT DU CARROUSEL) TAKE STEPS DOWN TO THE QUAY. AT THE NEXT BRIDGE (PONT ROYAL) GO UP THE STAIRS. EITHER WAY YOU WILL REACH MUSEE D'ORSAY.

Rue des Saints Peres is a premier street for **Le Carre de Rive Gauche**, an association of some 120 antique dealers and galleries with a spectrum of wares ranging from

Renaissance furniture to contemporary curios from East Africa. Association members post a discrete blue sign.

Quai Voltaire honors the penname of **Francois Marie Arouet**, who died in 1778 at #27 at age 83; Voltaire's prolific satire packed the wallop of a cable television station in its day. The block also attracted **Oscar Wilde**, who lived at #19, and writer-composer **Paul Bowles**, who left his upstairs apartment at #17 in 1931 and went to Morocco, where he would gather the grist for his later novel, *The Sheltering Sky*.

Musee d'Orsay, set in an ornate former railway station, has been a top-tier museum in Paris since it opened in 1986. Its collection includes works from 1848 to 1914, bridging the time spans covered by the Louvre's antiquities and the modern art of the Pompidou. You may not have time to do more than admire the statues and crowd scene in front, but a visit should be high on your list (an admission is charged).

Gare d'Orsay presciently was called "a fine arts palace" after its unveiling during the Exposition Universalle in 1900. But short platforms made it practically obsolete by 1937. The building alone is worth the price of admission. A grand hallway under a glass-and-wrought-iron ceiling 150 yards long covers 150,000 feet of floor space. A huge clock dominates the central gallery. All the big guns among Impressionists are well represented—Manet, Monet, Van Gogh, Renoir, Gauguin, Seurat, Cezanne, and so on. But don't overlook the Romanticists and Realists that led up to that style—Delacroix, Gustave Courbet, Eugene Boudin, and others. Stats: About 3 million people yearly visit Musee d'Orsay's 80 galleries that display 4,000 artworks.

END AT MUSEE D'ORSAY RER STATION, LINE C

MUSÉE DELACROIX

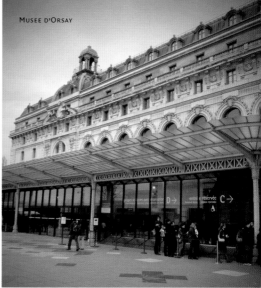

MUSEE D'ORSAY

QUAI VOLTAIRE

PLACE DE LA CONCORDE

WALKING TOUR FOUR

POSTCARDS

St. Eustache ... Forum des Halles ... Galerie Vero-Dodat ... Jardin du Palais Royal ... the vintage passages ... Folies Bergerie ... L'Opera Garnier... Galeries Lafayette ... Sainte Madeleine ... Rue du Faubourg St. Honore ... Place Vendome ... Place de la Concorde

THUMBNAIL:

This walk redefines "shopping." It starts at Forum des Halles, a modern underground mega-mall, which is next to the imposing church of St. Eustache. Then onto the gardens of Palais Royal, which at a turning point in history was a den of seedy commerce. The route then burrows through a half-dozen 18C enclosed alleys with shops and restaurants—the *passages* or *galeries*—the world's first malls. Then the fashion center of today's world comes alive on the streets around Sainte Madeleine and on the sprawling Rue du Faubourg St. Honore, the Broadway of haute couture. Staid Place Vendome (home of the Ritz) exudes wealth. The walk ends at Place de la Concorde, the busy heart of high-end Paris, where French royals and sympathizers knelt at the guillotine during the Revolution.

BIG PICTURE:

The length of Walking Tour Four will vary depending on the shortcuts and detours you decide to take. Nonetheless, you will have a full day of insight into the mind-boggling variety of high-end shopping on the Right Bank.

Distance: 4 to 5.5 miles   Time: 4 to 7.5 hours

Rue du Faubourg Saint-Honore

Palais Royal

St. Eustache

Passage Vero-Dodat

L'Opéra Garnier

Galeries Lafayette

Passage Jouffroy

Colonne Napoléon, Place Vendome

Sainte Madeline

WALKING TOUR
Four

START LES HALLES METRO STOP ON LINE 4.

FROM THE LES HALLES METRO, HEAD UP
RUE RAMBUTEAU TO ST. EUSTACHE, A LARGE
CHURCH THAT WILL BE ON YOUR RIGHT.

At the outer edge of the modern parks and
the enormous shopping complex at **Forum
des Halles** stands **St. Eustache**. This
church is second only to Notre Dame in
size and in breadth of cultural heritage. **Les
Halles** was a huge open-air marketplace
in Paris since forever. Covered stalls were
added in 1183 by King Philippe II Auguste.
In 1850 huge glass-and-wrought iron
buildings added permanency to "the belly
of Paris," as it was named in an Emile
Zola novel. But permanency fell prey to
changing economics and the market was
demolished in 1971. Vendors moved to the
suburb of Rungis and the subterranean
shopping complex was developed in the
mid-1970s. But St. Eustache remains as the
market quarter's soul.

Roman General Eustacious converted to
Christianity and built the small chapel
St. Agnes on this site in 532. For his
convictions, he and his family were burned
at the stake. In his honor, work on **St.
Eustache** began in 1532 and the church
was consecrated in 1637, a time span that
created a blend of Gothic and Renaissance
styles. A Romanesque façade was added
in 1754 and extensive renovation took
place in 1840. Inside, Flamboyant Gothic
vaulting creates 100-foot-high caverns in
the ceiling, and light beams down from
stained-glass masterworks. Aisles 330 feet
long are lined by massive columns. Details
in the naves and 24 chapels are more
disparate than the architecture. Included
are **The Tomb of Colbert** (an esteemed
17C political minister), an early painting
by P. P. Rubens, *Pilgrims at Emmaus*, and
a carved-metal triptych (three panels),

The Life of Christ, by modern artist **Keith
Haring** (1962-1990). Outside in **Place Rene
Cassin**, is a 10-foot sculpture of a head and
hand called **Ecoute** (Listen) by Henri de
Miller, a crowd pleaser since 1986.

FROM THE CHURCH, ANGLE RIGHT ACROSS
THROUGH THE PARK AND THEN HEAD TO
THE LEFT OF THE BLACK-DOMED BOURSE DU
COMMERCE. CROSS RUE DU LOUVRE, VEER LEFT
ON RUE JEAN-JACQUES ROUSSEAU, AND THEN
TURN RIGHT INTO GALERIE VERO-DODAT.

In the large **Jardins des Halles** are a
sunken children's park, walkways passing
conservatories with glass pyramids, and
a formal flower garden—a standout
park if this wasn't Paris. **The Bourse du
Commerce** is a former corn exchange that
got its metal dome in 1811. You'd never
guess that the stylish **Galerie Vero-Dodat**
was built as a butchery in 1826. Black-and-
white tiles and mahogany paneling gleam
in the light from overhead glazing that
runs its one block length. The shops are
elegantly sparing and include women's
shoes coveted by the ladies on TV's *Sex and
the City*. The first gas lighting in Paris was
in this arcade.

FROM THE GALERIE, CROSS THE STREET
AND GO STRAIGHT TO RUE MONTESQUIEU
AND CONTINUE THROUGH PASSAGE VERITE.
ENTER JARDIN DU PALAIS ROYAL.

The **Palais Royal** was the early 17C home
of Louis XIV's principal minister, **Cardinal
Richelieu**, reflecting the opulence of a time
when the monarchy was absolute. Striking
a discordant note at this entrance are
the arty striped stumps by Daniel Buren,
added in 1986 when modernistic accents
were popular. The palace was willed to the
crown, and became the childhood home to
Louis XIV, the Sun King. Debt plagued the
monarchy and in 1780 Philippe d'Orleans

added commercial arcades around the gardens—which degraded into gambling houses, seedy dance halls, and bordellos. In the late 18C the grounds were a meeting place that fomented the Revolution, and the then-owner of the Palais Royal, Prince Louis Philippe Egalite, was beheaded. In 1838 the grounds were a "hideous debauchery" that Sir Walter Scott, among others, wanted leveled.

Lime trees now adorn the open formal gardens and fountains of the palace, which is home to the Ministry of Culture. The arcades are home to chic boutiques and restaurants. Walk up the center and exit via the left side. You'll pass venerable **Le Grand Vefour**, where the rich and famous have dined since Napoleon was courting Josephine.

Detour: **Comedie Francaise** opened by Louis XIV in 1680, seven years after Moliere's death. Moliere's troupe had been performing in the east wing of the palace when the great actor-playwright collapsed on stage. The building is located on the southwest side of the Palais Royal (the part closest to the Seine).

WALK TO THE RIGHT, UP THE CENTER OF THE GARDENS, AND EXIT PALAIS ROYAL ON THE LEFT SIDE. GO RIGHT ON RUE DE BEAUJOLAIS, JOG LEFT BRIEFLY ON RUE VIVIENNE, AND THEN RIGHT ON RUE DES PETIT CHAMPS. ENTER AND EXIT GALERIE COLBERT. THEN WALK LEFT ON THE SIDEWALK AND ENTER GALERIE VIVIENNE.

At #9 **Rue de Beaujolais** (one of the original streets that enclosed the palace gardens) lived beloved writer **Sidonie Gabrielle Colette** (1873-1954), known simply by her surname. She wrote 50 semi-autobiographical novels about love life in Paris, including *Gigi* in 1944, which won nine Oscars when it was made into a movie four years after her death.

Immediately on your left on Rue des Petit Champs is **Galerie Colbert** of the Belle Époque period, with marble floors and an airy rotunda built in 1826. Featured inside are Le Grand Colbert restaurant and the elegant design studios used by the Sorbonne. Colbert was built due to the success of its neighbor a couple doors down, **Galerie Vivienne**, from 1823. Enter through the neoclassical stucco friezes and walk the marble-mosaic floors past esoteric boutiques, galleries, and antiquarian bookstores. The gallery makes a right-angle and drops to a lower section, all of it in the natural glow from skylights.

EXIT GALERIE VIVIENNE AND GO RIGHT ON RUE VIVIENNE. GO SEVERAL BLOCKS AND VEER RIGHT ON RUE FEYDEAU. GO LEFT ON RUE MONTMARTRE AND THEN IMMEDIATELY LEFT INTO GALERIE MONTMARTRE-PASSAGE DES PANORAMAS.

Across the street as you exit the Galerie Vivienne is **Bibliotheque Nationale**, the nation's storehouse for books, historic manuscripts, medals, and rare prints—although much material was moved in 1998 to Bibliotheque Mitterrand in Bercy (see Promenade Three, page 157). Areas are open to the public; enter on the opposite side from Rue de Richelieu. Farther up Vivienne on the right is the Roman temple-like **Bourse Stock Exchange**, where you can watch financial gladiators do battle from public seating areas.

Built in 1799, **Passage des Panoramas** was the first of about 100 pedestrian arcades in Paris, most with glass-vaulted ceilings and side galleries that allowed shopping

LES HALLES AND ST. EUSTACHE

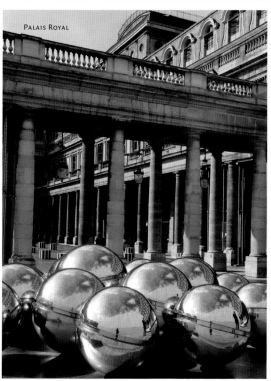

PALAIS ROYAL

GALERIE VIVIENNE

free of the rain. Some 20 of these "human aquariums" (as dubbed by a writer of the day) remain today. This passage has others that adjoin, added in the early 1800s; **galeries Feydeau** and **Montmartre** are on this end, and **Varieties** crosses in the center. People come to this complex for its large choice of ethnic restaurants and for stamps, antiquarian books, vintage photos, and post cards. At #47 is **Sterns**, which began in 1848 with royal commissions for hand-engraved cards and stationery.

FROM PASSAGE DES PANORAMAS, CROSS BLVD. MONTMARTRE AND ENTER PASSAGE JOUFFROY. EXIT AND CROSS RUE DE LA GRANGE BATELIERE AND ENTER PASSAGE VERDEAU.

Passage Jouffroy was the first to have heat, a big draw when it opened in 1845. Since 1882, its biggest attraction has been **Musee Grevin** (enter to the right of the passage), a wax museum with more than 250 figures ranging from Jimi Hendrix to Einstein to Marie Antoinette awaiting her fate from prison. The passage is brimming with handcrafted toys, ivory walking canes, miniatures, chocolates, antique weapons, and design baubles. Halfway through at #46 is **Hotel Chopin**, rated highly among budget travelers.

Passage Verdeau also opened with heat in 1845, but it is less glamorous. Its offerings include vintage books and postcards, lithographs, jewelry, bistros, and bric-a-brac. Galleries include **Cabinet des Curieux**, with psychosexual artwork that may arrest your stroll along the foot-worn marble.

EXIT PASSAGE VERDEAU, GO LEFT ON RUE DU FAUBOURG, AND THEN IMMEDIATELY LEFT ON RUE DE PROVENCE. THEN GO LEFT AT THE

NEXT STREET, RUE DROUOT. CONTINUE ON
DROUOT FOR SEVERAL BLOCKS AND CROSS
BLVD. MONTMARTRE. VEER RIGHT ON BUSY
BLVD. DES ITALIENS AND CONTINUE SEVERAL
BLOCKS TO L'OPERA.

Detour: To sneak a peep at **Folies Bergere**,
at the *passage* exit, cross Rue du Faubourg
Montmartre and then go right at Rue
Richer to address #32. The music hall
opened in 1869, decades before the Moulin
Rouge. It's heyday may have been from the
1890s to the Roaring Twenties, when the
big draw was scorching **Josephine Baker**.
But the Folies has remained a happening
place, where big name performers from W.
C. Fields to Elton John have had a gig.

If you have a half a million euros in loose
change, you might want to stop in at **Hotel
des Ventes** (#9 Rue Drouot) and buy some
fine art at auction. This establishment
is the Sotheby's of Paris. *Detour:* From
Boulevard des Italiens, jog left one block
at Rue de Marivaux to see **Opera Comique**,
set in charming Place Boieldieu. This
light-hearted theatre originated in 17C
street fairs, but moved to this ornate, 1,200
seat theater in 1783. Opera Comique's
greatest production, *Carmen*, bombed
when first produced in 1875—the story of
an amorous, ill-fated Gypsy was mocked by
audiences and critics alike. Author George
Bizet died without knowing *Carmen* would
take the rest of Europe by storm—thus
changing the nature of this form of
theater—and stage a triumphant return
to Paris in 1883. Of other note in the *place*:
The painter **Francisco Goya** lived in 1824 at
Hotel Favart.

Boulevard des Italiens ends at busier **Place
l'Opera** in front of the massive and ornate
Opera de Paris Garnier. Built over 14 years
beginning in 1861 by architect Jean Garnier,
the opera is a mishmash of Baroque and

neo-Renaissance styles typical of Napoleon III's Second Empire. The huge staircase in front is a traditional meeting place, surrounded by majestic columns rising to gilded figures and numerous friezes that decorate the façade. An underground lake was discovered during construction, which became the inspiration for *Phantom of the Opera*, a 1910 novel by Gaston Leroux.

The visiting entrance is around to the left side of the building; an admission is charged. The interior **Grand Staircase** opens at the **Grand Foyer**, both amid a symphony of gilded decoration, mirrors, and frescoes. Of special note are a ceiling painted by **Marc Chagall** and a six-ton chandelier. The sprawling stage holds some 450 performers, but only 2,200 spectators can fill the five-tier auditorium. Mitterrand commissioned a larger opera house to be built in Bastille in 1989.

FROM THE BACK OF OPERA GARNIER, GO UP RUE SCRIBE AND CROSS BLVD. HAUSSMANN TO GALERIES LAFAYETTE.

The granddame of department stores, **Galeries Lafayette** opened in 1898. Its acres of floor space catered to the new bourgeois. The store is in two huge buildings, separated by Rue Mogador, which abuts Boulevard Haussmann. Enter the right-side building and go to the third floor to see the store's centerpiece. A grandiose Belle Époque dome, 100 feet in diameter, is ringed by balustrades on several floors that reveal views of lavish shopping at its best. Then head to the rooftop (via an elevator to the sixth floor and an escalator near the restaurant) for one of the city's great freebie views. *Detour:* After leaving Galeries Lafayette, go a block farther down Boulevard Haussmann to see this store's older rival **Au Printemps**, founded in 1865. Printemps is not as splashy for tourists, but Parisians form opinions over which is best, sort of like Coke and Pepsi.

GO BACK ACROSS BLVD. AND BACKTRACK DOWN RUE SCRIBE PAST THE OPERA. THEN GO RIGHT ONTO BLVD. DES CAPUCINES. PASS RUE DE CAUMARTIN AND VEER RIGHT ON RUE DE SEZE. CONTINUE TO PLACE DE LA MADELEINE.

In his exuberance after winning the 1805 Battle of Austerlitz against a Russo-Austrian coalition, Napoleon envisioned a Temple of Glory for the Grande Armee. But he was long gone before **Sainte Madeleine** was completed in 1842. From a forest of Corinthian columns of this larger-than-Greek temple, you can sit atop a run of stairs and look upon one leg of the **Axis of Historique**: The view is down Rue Royale and across Place de la Concorde to Palais Bourbon on the other side the Seine. (The other arm of the axis, from Arc de Triomphe to the Louvre, intersects at right angles in the middle of Place de la Concorde.)

The interior of **Sainte Madeleine** is all about symmetry as well. A single nave and semi-circular choir are lit dimly by skylights, which also draw attention to three ceiling domes with bas-reliefs of the Apostles. The church's first ceremonial glory was the memorial to **Frederic Chopin** in 1849, when thousands of mourners heard the debut of his "Funeral March," as well as a performance by Franz Liszt. Madeleine's greatest day perhaps was in 1975 at a tribute to American-born **Josephine Baker**, who had captivated Paris since coming here to live 50 years earlier. She is most remembered for her torrid singing and dancing in the Roaring Twenties, when she became a muse for a long list of the best-known artists and writers of the day. After WWII, the beautiful

OPERA GARNIER

OPERA COMIQUE

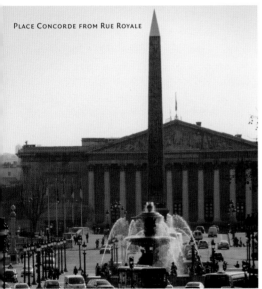
PLACE CONCORDE FROM RUE ROYALE

GALERIES LAFAYETTE ROOFTOP

AU PRINTEMPS

PLACE DE LA MADELINE

Baker won a medal of honor from France for her efforts in the Resistance. In the ensuing decades, she was involved in the effort to racially integrate the performance arts and—incredibly—was offered leadership of the Civil Rights movement in 1968 by Coretta Scott King, after the King assassination.

Place de la Madeleine is a Mecca for gourmets, set appropriately at the edge of the haute couture quarter. Behind the church on Rue de Seze is **Fauchon**, home to mouthwatering pleasures from caviar to chocolates that have lured Parisians since 1886. The displays are works of art. Nearby, in business since 1854, is its rival **Hediard**, also boasting the best—of everything. Other shops on the street will vie for your attention, including **Marquise de Sevigne**, where chocolates are a way of life. On the east side of Madeleine are flower stalls (of course, to go with the delicacies). A touch of economy amid extravagance on the west side is the **Kiosque Theatre**, where theater tickets can be purchased for half-price on the day of the performance.

STAND WITH YOUR BACK TO THE FRONT OF MADELEINE AND GO RIGHT, CROSSING BUSY BLVD. MALESHERBES. ON THE RIGHT IS GALERIE DE LA MADELEINE. CONTINUE STRAIGHT DOWN RUE ROYAL.

At #160 Malesherbes is the residence of **Coco Chanel** when she was new to the fashion scene at age 25. Her bang-cut hair and trim-fit fashions put an end to the corsets and parasols after the turn of the twentieth century. On your right are chances to duck into two fashion passages, **Galerie de la Madeleine**, where not much has changed since the 1800s, and, just after that, **Cite Berryer**, another enclosed gallery of shops and restaurants that was renovated in 1994.

FROM RUE ROYAL, GO RIGHT ON RUE DU FAUBOURG-ST. HONORE.

Beginning as a medieval dirt road from Paris to the village of Roule, **Rue du Faubourg-St. Honore** became fashionable early, under reign of Louis IV. Today it is the prime address for high-end fashion designers. You'll find elegant hotels, embassies, state residences, and a who's who in the world of fashion lining both sides of the street. Look for Versace, Saint Laurent, Guy Laroche, Cardin, Dior, Cartier, Hermes, Chanel, Prada, Lancôme, Ungaro, Valentino, Ferregamo, Givenchy, and newcomers who are making it big.

WALK UP RUE DU FAUBOURG-ST. HONORE, PICK A TURN-AROUND, AND DOUBLE BACK TO RUE ROYALE.

Along Faubourg-St. Honore, look for **House of Lanvin** at #22, which was set up by Jeanne Lanvin in 1890, an early benchmark in haute couture elegance. **Hermes** is at #24, worth a look to see the saddles that were an early trademark. At #29 is a former residence of **Coco Chanel** in 1925, where she kept an extra room for buddy **Pablo Picasso**.

The **British Embassy** is located at #35, the birthplace of author **Somerset Maugham**, giving him an early start on a globetrotting career. The armed police you may see outside #55 are guarding the French President, who sometimes resides at the huge grounds of the **Palais de l'Elysee**. Farther down at #118 is where **Pierre Cardin** worked for **Christian Dior** in the 1950s, before launching an empire of stores in 100 countries—a move that became the trend among haute couture houses.

AFTER DOUBLING BACK ON FAUBOURG-ST. HONORE, CROSS RUE ROYAL AND CONTINUE FOR THREE BLOCKS AS THE ROUTE BECOMES RUE ST. HONORE FOR THREE BLOCKS. GO LEFT ON RUE CASTIGLIONE TO PLACE VENDOME. NOTE: IF YOU WANT TO SHORTEN THE TOUR, GO RIGHT ON RUE ROYAL TO PLACE DE LA CONCORDE.

The aroma of perfumed money wafts the 300-yard expanse of cobblestones at **Place Vendome**, among the most chi-chi and mighty of Parisian addresses since it was laid out in 1702. But this square of uniformly arcaded facades has not lacked turmoil. An equestrian statue of Louis XIV was torn down after the monarchy fell. A statue of the emperor atop **Colonne Napoleon** was toppled in 1871, when Napoleon III was living out the last 20 years of his life in seclusion on the upper level of #26. The current 144-foot-high bronze column, which rises in a spiral of friezes, was modeled after Rome's Trajan and was made from 1,200 enemy cannons that were captured at the Battle of Austerlitz.

The most illustrious landmark on **Place Vendome** is the hotel at #15, opened in 1898 by Cesar Ritz. Poet Andre Farque observed some 20 years later, "And what do rich girls dream about? And what is Paris? The Ritz." Coco Chanel lived here at the time of her death, F. Scott and Zelda raved of the private baths, and Hemingway held down a stool so often he got the bar named after himself. **Fred Astaire** preferred Hotel Vendome during visits in the late 1930s. **J. P. Morgan** roughed it at Hotel Bristol during his stays, around 1910. Composer **Chopin's** death bed in 1849 was at his residence at #12. Residing currently on the *place* are Dior, Chanel, DeBeers, Cartier and other purveyors of keepsake bling.

Detour: Over the years, celebrities have wandered from Vendome to nearby **Harry's Bar**. Go a short two blocks north from Vendome on Rue de la Paix and walk right on Rue Daunou to address #5. Bellied up to the bar have been James Joyce, Thornton Wilder, Charlie Chaplain, Gloria Swanson, Noel Coward, Jack Dempsey, Hemingway—and so on.

EXIT THE SOUTH END OF PLACE VENDOME ON RUE DE CASTIGLIONE. GO RIGHT ON RUE DE RIVOLI AND CONTINUE PAST PLACE DE LA CONCORDE TO RUE BOISSY D'ANGLAS.

At #7 Rue Castiglione is **Hotel Lotti**, were **George Orwell** worked as a dishwasher in 1919, a task that inspired his 1933 book, *Down and Out in Paris and London*. Running alongside the Louvre, **Rue de Rivoli** was created in the early 1800s for high-class promenading. With mosaic sidewalks and stone arcades, it still suits that purpose, though T-shirt-and-trinket shops mingle with the finer stores.

On your right as you reach Rue Royale is **Hotel de la Marine**, with an ornately colonnaded façade that dates from 1757. The building's interior, now used by the French Navy, is equally elaborate. **Rue Royale**, which connects the Madeleine to Concorde, was built in the early 18C by Louis XIII. During the grandiose Belle Époque (late 19C to the beginning of WWI) it evolved to become the center of fashion.

Across Rue Royale are two of Paris's swankest establishments. On the right at #3 is **Maxim's**, a rococo restaurant that began as an eat house for cabbies but became home to the chic and the decadent in the early 1900s. Writers like Sinclair Lewis and F. Scott Fitzgerald added panache to a clientele sprinkled with classy courtesans. The club remains popular, albeit in a more mainstream way. Prominent on the corner is **Hotel Crillon**, the architecturally lavish, near twin of Hotel de la Marine, is arguably the most prestigious place to stay in Paris. It was here that the Treaty of Friendship was signed by Louis XV in 1778, recognizing the independence of the 13 states and giving impetus to the American Revolution. Crillon went Hollywood in the 1920s, buoyed by the honeymoon of Douglas Fairbanks and Mary Pickford. Movie stars like Kristen Stewart, etc., keep Crillon current, but the place remains "French" enough to snub even well-known directors who order a Coke with a gourmet meal. The U. S. connection is furthered by the **American Embassy**, which is on Boissy just past the Crillon.

DOUBLE BACK FROM RUE BOISSY D'ANGLAS AND TAKE A CROSSWALK TO PLACE DE LA CONCORDE.

Place de la Concorde is meant to be seen from the center of its 20-plus acres. So brave the multiple lanes of screaming traffic and make the dash at the crosswalk. You will find the 3,300-year-old **Obelisk of Luxor**, 230 tons of pink granite rising about 70 feet, a gift in 1829 from the pasha of Egypt. The spire took four years to travel to Paris. Etched into the stone are hieroglyphics telling of the exploits of the pharaohs. Prior to that, the *place's* centerpiece was a guillotine, which severed the heads Marie Antoinette, Louis XVI, Robespierre, and some 1,300 other souls during the Revolution in 1793. What had been Place de la Concorde since it was laid out in 1755 by Louis XV became Place de la Revolution for a few years.

Concorde is also at the center of the **Axis Historique**, known widely among urban planners as "the most beautiful

OBELISK OF LUXOR

architectural ensemble on the planet." The vast line of symmetry stretches from La Defense and Arc de Triomphe to the Louvre, and intersects at 90 degrees with a line from Sainte Madeleine to Palais Bourbon. Next to Bourbon is, Assemblee Nationale, home to the French Parliament since 1798, except when the Germans took over from 1940 to 1944. The eight statue groups at Place de la Concorde, honoring cities of France, were placed by King Louis Philippe in 1795. The extravagant nautical fountains—**Fontaine des Fleuves** and **Fontaine des Mers**—were added in 1840, modeled after ones in Rome's St. Peter's Square.

END AT CONCORDE METRO STOP FOR LINES 1, 8, AND 12.

PLACE GEORGES POMPIDOU

WALKING TOUR FIVE

POSTCARDS:

Hotel de Ville ... Tour St. Jacques ... Rue St. Martin ... Centre Georges Pompidou ... Fontaine des Innocents ... Musee des Arts et Metiers ... Porte St. Martin ... Rue Saint Denis ... Passage du Caire ... Marche Montorgeuil ... Tour Jean Sans Peur

THUMBNAIL:

The edgy and the elegant blend in a walk that takes in the no-nonsense wholesale fashion districts, street life, and classic monuments. Hotel de Ville is steeped in tradition, while fanciful Pompidou museum celebrates modernity. Streets and *passages* in these neighborhoods are where buyers come from all over the world. Hookers of St. Denis stand alongside garment workers wheeling bolts of fabric. Rue Montorgeuil is street life personified, with historic cafés and shops to tickle taste buds.

BIG PICTURE:

Starting with the grand city center at Hotel de Ville, this walk is a behind-the-scenes look at the glamour of Paris. Certain parts of the tour, though perfectly safe, may not be right for (or of interest to) children. Montorgeuil is an epicurean's delight, a sure thing to enjoy at day's end.

DISTANCE: 3 to 3.5 miles   TIME: 2.5 to 4.5 hours

HOTEL DE VILLE

MUSÉE DES ARTS ET METIERS

MUSEE POMPIDOU

Tour St. Jacques

Rue Montorgueil

Porte St. Martin

RUE DES MARTYRS

PASSAGE GRAND CERF

WALKING TOUR
Five

START AT HOTEL DE VILLE METRO STOP, LINES 1 AND 11.

WALK TO THE FRONT ENTRANCE OF HOTEL DE VILLE. WALK AWAY FROM THE HOTEL ON AVE. VICTORIA AND TURN RIGHT ON RUE. ST. MARTIN.

Hotel de Ville stands at what was formerly **Place de Greve**, the largest square in the city in the 1300s. The *place* hosted both rowdy merrymaking and rowdier public executions. In 1610, Henry IV's assassin, Ravaillac, had hot lead poured in open wounds before his limbs were pulled apart by horses. You'll find a statue of provost **Etienne Marcel**, who in 1358 led the Third Estate (the emerging merchants and middle class) in rallies against the monarchy. The current Hotel de Ville was built over a 19-year span beginning in 1873 and is now city hall for Paris. Its neo-Renaissance style reflects the splendor of the Third Republic, with a façade that includes 300-plus works of art and niches that hold statues of eminent Frenchmen. The interior has a series of beautiful reception halls, gleaming chandeliers, gilded filigree, ornate woodwork, and a sumptuous staircase.

A gateway to Hotel de Ville, **Avenue Victoria** is a popular venue for loudly choreographed political demonstrations, a still-thriving French tradition. **Tour St. Jacques** (1512) sparkles from a recent cleaning. The Flamboyant Gothic, 170-foot-high bell tower in the center of the greenspace is all that remains of the church Saint Jacques de la Boucherie. In the 16C, this was a starting point for pilgrimages to Santiago, Spain. Across Rue de Rivoli, **Rue St. Martin** becomes cobblestones for pedestrians only. It was a major route built by the Romans.

CONTINUE UP RUE ST. MARTIN, TURN RIGHT AT THE CHURCH ON SMALL RUE DU CLOITRE ST. MERRI. THEN GO LEFT AND PASS THE FOUNTAIN OF PLACE IGOR STRAVINSKY TO CENTRE GEORGES POMPIDOU.

Small **St. Merri**, built over 35 years beginning in 1515, replaced other churches from the 7C. Mainly Flamboyant Gothic in style, its northwest turret holds the oldest bell in Paris, ringing since 1331. With the Pompidou rising in the background, you may not focus on the whimsical sheet of water that is **Fontaine Igor Stravinsky**, with 16 multicolored mobiles and several spurting sculptures. The surrounding plaza is a gathering place for street artists and performers.

Critics and fans alike have many zesty nicknames for this 1977 Parisian art project, but rarely the full name of **Pompidou Centre Musee National d'Art Moderne**. Like a building turned inside out—or some benign factory as drawn in a comic book—the Pompidou's glass façade reveals its massive colorful ducting and infrastructure. Big blue tubes pipe air, the green ones hold water, and the yellow are stuffed with electrical and communications cables. Escalators in translucent tubes are arteries that transport people on a zigzagging ride up five floors. The red elevator adds zip to the price of admission as does a trip for the view from the avante garde restaurant terrace on top, Le Georges.

Having the infrastructure hanging on the exterior, aside from being visually amusing, allows for a huge amount of interior space—200,000 square feet. Entrance to the expansive foyer is free. The **Pompidou's galleries** hold masterpieces of art from 1905 to the present, completing the full spectrum of time that begins with the Louvre, which is followed by Musee d'Orsay. The collection runs the gamut, if there is one, from Cubism, to Surrealism, to Pop Art, and includes esoteric offshoots like the Expressionists and Dada. All the big guns are exhibited, including Picasso, Matisse, Magritte, Miro, Dali, Paul Klee, Calder, Kadinsky, and Jackson Pollock.

WITH THE POMPIDOU AT YOUR BACK, WALK TO THE LEFT ACROSS THE PLAZA ONTO RUE AUBREY LE BOUCHER. THEN GO RIGHT ON RUE QUINCAMPOIX. JOG RIGHT ON RUE RAMBUTEAU AND THEN GO LEFT ONTO RUE SAINT MARTIN.

Detour: Continue on Rue Boucher two short blocks past Rue Quincampoix to see **Fontaine des Innocents**. After all the modernity, this kiosk with delicate bas-reliefs may be a welcome blast from the past. Built in 1549, it is the only Renaissance fountain in Paris. Its steep tiers of steps are a meeting place. After sitting a spell with your new French friends, double back to Quincampoix.

Street art is a continued theme on Rue Quincampoix, with alleys that open toward Pompidou. Same on Rue Saint Martin, centered around enticing **Passage Moliere**. Just past the passage, jog right into a courtyard to see **l'Horloge a Automates le Defenseur du Temps**, the "Defender of Time Clock" that lurches alive on the hour (noon is the best show). Hanging from the wall is a four-foot high ton of brass, supporting a Quixotic figure wearing armor who does eternal battle with earthquakes, hurricanes, and other natural furies.

FROM ST. MARTIN, GO RIGHT ON RIGHT ON RUE MONTMORENCY, LEFT ON WIDE RUE BEAUBOURG, AND THEN RIGHT ON RUE CHAPON. FROM CHAPON, GO LEFT THROUGH PASSAGE DE GRAVILLIERS, EMERGE, JOG RIGHT, AND THEN LEFT INTO RUE DES VERTUS.

You now leave touristville for a swing through the workaday world of wholesale fashion and accessories—overlaid upon some of the ancient streets of Paris. At #51 Rue Montmorency is **La Maison de Nicolas Flamel**, the oldest private home in the city, dating from 1407. Angels flutter upon its façade. On **Rue Chapon** are drably set store windows heaped with wallets, purses, and luggage—*vente en gros*—sold by the dozen. Cafes and no-frills galleries are also in the mix. Gritty **Passage de Gravilliers** dates from the 13C. **Rue des Vertus** (virtue) was named as a pun, since prostitutes frequented the street in the old days, but now voices of children from a local school fill the air. Trade buyers will have more chances to buy handbags by the dozen and fill them with costume jewelry.

FROM VERTUS, GO LEFT ON BUSY RUE REAUMUR, CROSS TURBIGO, AND THEN GO RIGHT ONTO RUE VAUCANSON.

The shop windows of **Rue Reaumur** also are loaded with necklaces and jewelry. Fashion world ends abruptly across Turbigo, at **the Musee des Arts et Metiers**. The mechanically minded will love this place. An admission is charged. Outside, the gleaming engine of a French TGV bullet train is set incongruously in the courtyard of the 13C Gothic church, **Saint Martin des Champs**. Inside are a broad range of tools, instruments, and machines. Started by an abbot in 1794, the collection consists of about 80,000 objects and 15,000 drawings. The museum traces the evolution of technology by showing visitors the real deal, such as Guttenberg's printing device from 1438, Pascal's 1642 calculating machine, and an Edison phonograph that dates from 1877.

Rue Reumur

Maison de Nicolas Flamel

Pompidou Centre

Rue des Vertus

Fontaine Igor Stravinsky and St. Merri

PASSAGE DU CAIRE

MUSÉE DES ARTS ET MÉTIERS

RUE DU NIL

PORTE ST. DENIS

RUE ST. DENIS

FROM VAUCANSON, GO RIGHT ON RUE
VERTBOIS, THEN LEFT ON RUE VOLTA, AND
STRAIGHT THROUGH PASSAGE DU PONT AUX
BICHES. AT RUE MESLAY, JOG RIGHT, AND
THEN GO LEFT INTO PASSAGE MESLAY. CROSS
BUSY BLVD. ST. MARTIN, AND THEN GO LEFT
ON RUE RENE BOULANGER. VEER RIGHT AT
BUSY BLVD. ST. DENIS (ST. MARTIN).

Don't be surprised to see someone
sleeping in the street as you climb the
stairs at **Passage du Pont aux Biches**—
which dates from 1881, when it was a
bridge with a sign of a deer. **Passage
Meslay**, opened seven years later, is more
practical than interesting, although it
is artfully memorialized by 1909 photos
by **Eugene Atget**. The passage opens to
Place Johann Strauss (there's a bust)
where you cross St. Martin. **Rue Rene
Boulanger** dates from 1771, but it was
not named for the French Resistance hero
until 1994. The street curves through a
lively neighborhood of shops, cafes, and
ethnic restaurants. At #17 is the site of
the international school set up by **Marcel
Marceau**, the famous mime artist.

The beginning of Boulevard St. Denis is
announced by the 55-foot high **Porte
St. Martin**. The marble-and-limestone
arch was erected in 1674 by Louis XIV (on
the site of a medieval gate to the city) to
commemorate military victories on the
Rhine. Same goes for **Porte St. Denis**,
two blocks farther down the boulevard:
It replaces a gate in the city wall during
the reign of Charles V, and was erected by
Louis XIV as a shrine to the same wars. But
the St. Denis arch is on a Roman scale, 20
feet higher and decorated with bas-reliefs
of allegorical figures and battle scenes.
It lies on the major Roman route leading
north from Lutetia (Paris), which was also
the processional route into Paris of Queen
Victoria in 1855.

AT PORTE ST. DENIS, GO LEFT DOWN RUE ST.
DENIS. AFTER A COUPLE BLOCKS, GO RIGHT
THROUGH PASSAGE DU CAIRE. EMERGE AND
GO AROUND LEFT THROUGH SMALL PLACE DU
CAIRE. TAKE A LEFT FROM THE PLACE ON RUE
DE DAMIETTE, AND THEN A QUICK RIGHT ON
SMALL RUE DU NIL.

Aside from the hubbub of normal
commerce, the procession of street
workers on **Rue St. Denis** are of two
types: men in overalls with hand-trucks
transporting bolts of fabric, and "ladies
of the night," who are spaced evenly in
broad daylight along the sidewalk and
tarted-up like Christmas trees. Parisians
seem to take little note of either (no photos
without permission). You might want to
continue down Rue St. Denis a little before
doubling back to slightly shabby **Passage
du Caire**. Crowds of nude mannequins and
all sorts of shelving and racks are behind
the windows of this long *passage*, which
supplies retail stores.

When exiting to **Place du Caire**, turn
around to take note of the Egyptian-head
decorations that were placed in 1798 to
honor Napoleon's earlier victories in Cairo.
It's common in this small *place* to see
boutique owners making big buys, with
workers pushing dolly-loads behind them
to be transported to nearby vans—and
thence to ready-to-wear stores throughout
the world. Re-entry from the workaday
world back into elegant Paris may be
marked at #5 Rue du Nil, at **Frenchie**, an
uber-cool restaurant that is barely signed
and where reservations can only be made
by phone during certain hours. The food
backs up its popularity.

FROM RUE DU NIL, GO LEFT ON RUE DES
PETITS CARREAUX AND CONTINUE AS IT
BECOMES RUE MONTORGEUIL.

Across Rue Reaumur, the green-ironwork archway of **Marche Montorgeuil** welcomes gourmets and everybody else to a mind-boggling ensemble for the taste buds—and all of it artfully presented along a historic cobblestone street closed to traffic. Claude Monet captured the market's essence in a painting that hangs in Musee d'Orsay. Forget about boutiques and galleries. Montorgeuil is about the palate. This is particularly true at **Strohrer's** at #51, where pastries are (almost) too beautiful to eat. Nicholas Strohrer baked for Louis XV at Versailles and moved to this location in 1730. **Julien Davin**, the boucherie at #71, will entice carnivores, and, to go with it, try the breads at **Le Fournil de Pierre**, one of several locations. At #78 is **Au Rocher du Cancale**, where Balzac and Stendhal would belly up to the zinc bar and eat oysters in the mid-1800s.

FROM MONTORGEUIL, GO LEFT ON RUE MARIE STUART AND CONTINUE STRAIGHT INTO PASSAGE GRAND CERF. EMERGE, TURN RIGHT ON RUE ST. DENIS AND THEN IMMEDIATELY RIGHT ON RUE TIQUETONNE. (YOU MAY WANT TO SEE MORE DOWN MONTOGEUIL AND COME BACK TO STUART.)

Intimate **Rue Marie Stuart** was named in 1809 for the woman better known as Mary, Queen of Scots—widowed after one year of marriage in 1560 with the death of Francis II. Before honoring the queen, the rue was named for the sausage pulling that went on in this medieval market district. The street ends at **Passage du Grand Cerf**, a reference to a large stag that furthers the meat theme. Today the passage, with carved maidens at its entrance, is an elegant setting (tile floors, wood paneling, iron-work skylights) for three-dozen shops with artisan jewelry, imported art, and small boutiques. Turn right from the passage and then right again onto narrow **Rue Tiquetonne**. The curving cobblestones are along the former section of the 14C wall around Paris built by Philippe Auguste. The quaint street is also the literary home to d'Artagnan, one of the characters in Alexandre Dumas's *Three Musketeers*.

GO LEFT ON RUE FRANCAISE AND IMMEDIATELY LEFT ON RUE ETIENNE MARCEL.

Tour Jean Sans Peur (John the Fearless) is the ironic name for the Duke of Burgundy, who in 1409 built this defensive tower at his compound along the old city wall. An admission is charged. As part of the Hundred Years War, he had killed the brother of the king, an act that earned him his own assassination. The stairs that spiral upward through several floors of the tour reveal interesting details of the times (the latrine for instance), but don't expect a view from the top.

END AT ETIENNE MARCEL METRO STOP, LINE 4. THE ENTRANCE IS TO THE LEFT AT THE JUNCTION WITH RUE DE TURBIGO.

Au Rocher du Cancale

Passage du Caire

Tour Jean Sans Peur

Marche Montorgeuil

PLACE DES VOSGES

WALKING TOUR SIX

POSTCARDS:

Hotel de Sully ... Place des Vosges ... Maison de Victor Hugo ... The Marais ... Rue des Rosiers ... Archives Nationales ... Musee de la Chasse et de Nature ... Square du Temple ... Marche Infants Rouge ... Musee Carnavalet ... Musee Picasso ... Village St. Paul ... Hotel de Sens

THUMBNAIL:

The walk takes in some of Paris's excellent-but-unheralded museums, including homages to Victor Hugo and Pablo Picasso. Village life in the Marais is revealed—both ancient and contemporary. Cobbled streets wind pass galleries, markets, and park squares.

BIG PICTURE:

Though in the thick of the city, the rhythm of this tour is set by times gone by—many centuries past in places.

DISTANCE: 2.5 to 3 miles   TIME: 3.5 to 5.5 hours

ARCHIVES NATIONALES

THE MARAIS

MUSÉE CARNAVALET

HÔTEL DE JEAN LOUIS RAOUL

RUE CHARLOT

SQUARE DU TEMPLE

Impasse de la Poissonnerie

Maison de Victor Hugo

Rue de Sevigne and St. Louis-St. Paul

WALKING TOUR
Six

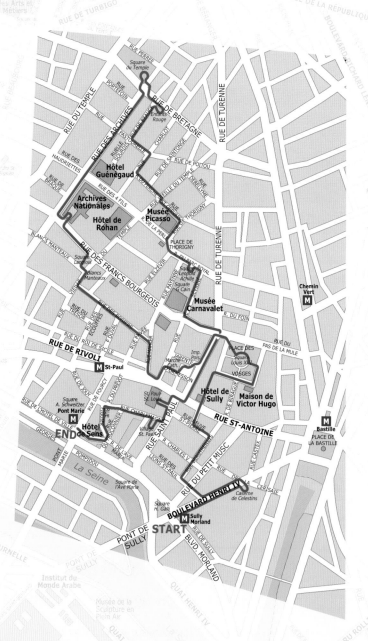

START AT THE SULLY-MORLAND METRO STOP, LINE 7.

WALK AWAY FROM THE RIVER, UP BLVD. HENRY IV.

The Seine used to flow where Boulevard Morland is today, making a third central island called **Ile de Louviers**. The flood-prone land, which was used for timber and as pasture, was made part of the Right Bank in 1843 when the river was filled to make the boulevard. At the small **Square Henri Galli** (across Blvd. Henry IV) you can find chunks of the infamous Bastille prison that were discovered while excavating for the St. Antoine metro.

At #22 Boulevard Henry IV is **Caserne des Celestins**, home to 600 mounted police who patrol the huge parks of Paris. Though the barracks are not a tourist attraction, the guard will let you peer in. If the timing is right, the bugle corps will be practicing with the uniformed cavalry. The academy is on the site of a monastery built in 1362.

DOUBLE-BACK ON BLVD. HENRY IV, CROSS TO THE RIGHT AT RUE DES LIONS ST. PAUL. GO RIGHT AGAIN ON RUE BEAUTRELLIS, LEFT ON RUE NEUVE ST. PIERRE, AND THEN RIGHT ON RUE L' HOTEL ST. PAUL. CROSS RUE SAINT ANTOINE AND ENTER HOTEL DE SULLY.

The old door at #6 Rue Beautrellis is the **Hotel de Jean Louis Raoul**, a 17C mansion. Of more recent historical note is the flat at #17, where **Jim Morrison** of the Doors was found dead in 1971, a result of drug use combined with a heart condition. Some say he died at a local club and was moved here. He'd spent the previous night on the Left Bank, in the apartment where Oscar Wilde stayed. (Morrison is buried at Pere Lachaise, along with Wilde; see Promenade Four, page 159.)

The Duke of Sully was 74 when he wowed society in 1632 by decorating his young wife with diamonds and moved into the stylish **Hotel de Sully**, a mansion of Louis XIII-late-Renaissance style. The duke, a high-level minister of King Henry IV, died there, but not before his wife could entertain a lover or two. Between the mansion's two pavilions is a large courtyard for carriages, with carved female statuary in four corners meant to represent the elements of nature. Four matching males, hanging around in the corners with the women, depict the four seasons. A vine that covers one wall functions as an aviary for small birds. Hotel de Sully opens onto what was then the Royal Palace (and now Places des Vosges), adding to its splendor among the mansions in the Marais. You'll find an excellent bookstore here.

GO THROUGH THE BACK OF HOTEL DE SULLY AND ENTER PLACE VOSGES.

Commissioned in 1604 by bon vivant **Henry IV**, **Place des Vosges** is the oldest square in Paris. Rising from the swamplands of the Marais to be the new Royal Palace, it is a study in symmetry, with four sides lined by nine townhouses with steep slate roofs, brick facades, and a gallery of walking arcades. Henry IV was assassinated two years before completion, and the square's inaugural event was the wedding of **Louis XIII** to **Anne of Austria** in 1612.

Go right as you enter the *place* and in the corner you'll find its most popular destination, **Maison de Victor Hugo**. France's most celebrated author (and that's saying something) lived here from 1832 to 1848, during which time he composed *Les Miserables*. Sumptuous decorations complement drawings and other works by Hugo, covering several floors. Admission is free (though renting an audio tape is very useful). The residence was made a museum in 1903, eight years after Hugo's death.

During the Revolution, **Place des Vosges** was renamed Place of Indivisibility and made a home for craftspeople. But a renovation took place in 1870 and it was renamed Place des Vosges, and the **Statue of Louis XIII**, smirking on horseback, was placed at its center. You may wish to explore the low-key galleries and restaurants, or to sit and contemplate it all from one of many benches amid leafy trees.

EXIT PLACE DES VOSGES CATER-CORNER FROM MAISON HUGO, AT PAVILION DE LA REINE. TURN LEFT ON RUE DE TURENNE AND THEN RIGHT ON SMALL RUE DE JARENTE. WALK LEFT THROUGH PLACE DU MARCHE STE. CATHERINE TO RUE D'ORMESSON.

At #2 Rue Jarente is **Impasse de la Poissonnerie**, a 20- by 50-foot cubbyhole that was a through street in 1783, when the fountain inside was built. As the name and bas-reliefs of dolphins and fish suggest, the site was where seafood was cleaned.

Continuing past the fountain, on the left is **Place du Marche Sainte Catherine**, an irresistibly charming square that dates from the 13C—although surrounding buildings were built mostly in the 18C. Ringed by cafes and restaurants, the shaded square draws tourists and Parisians alike. **Rue d'Ormesson** may be recognizable to Matt Damon and fans of The Bourne Identity movie, scenes of which were filmed here.

GO RIGHT ON D'ORMESSON, AND LEFT ON RUE DE SEVIGNE TO BUSY RUE DE RIVOLI. GO RIGHT AND THEN IMMEDIATELY RIGHT AGAIN ON RUE MAHLER. AFTER A BLOCK, WALK LEFT ON RUE DES ROSIERS.

In the 13C King Louis Philippe expelled the Jewish population of Paris to outside the newly built walls, and since then **Rue des Rosiers** in the Marais has been the "Pletzl" (Little Place) for the community. At the beginning, Rue des Rosiers crosses **Rue Pavee**, the first street with cobblestones in Paris, laid in the 13C. Traces of the old Louis Philippe wall can be seen at addresses #8, #10, and #14.

Rosiers narrows and curves through newer boutiques and kosher shops. A line usually forms at #32, **L'as du Fallafel**, which some say is the best Middle Eastern food in Paris. **Sasha Finkelstein**, at #27, is equally popular for its Yiddish baked goods. To the right off Rue des Rosiers (at #6 Rue des Hospitalieres-St. Gervais) is the Jewish school, **Espace Blancs Manteaux**, from which the Nazis deported some 165 children to war camps during WWII.

FROM ROSIERS, JOG RIGHT ON RUE VIEILLE DU TEMPLE AND THEN IMMEDIATELY LEFT ON RUE DES BLANCS MANTEAUX. THEN WALK RIGHT THROUGH THE LITTLE PARK, SQUARE CHARLES VICTOR LANGLOIS, AND GO LEFT ON RUE DES FRANCIS BOURGEOIS.

Shaded by birch and Hawthorne trees, the new (1961) neighborhood park of **Square Charles Victor Langlois** is the spot to take a rest. Or, stop for lunch at **Le Dome du Marais** (#53 bis Rue Francs Bourgeois), set in a renovated Louis XVIII-era chapel, which features a courtyard and winter garden to compliment its signature dome.

The main event on this street is at #60, **Hotel de Soubise**, which houses a branch of the **Archives Nationales** as well as the **Musee de l'Historie de France**. The hotel is an early-18C renovation for the Princess of Soubise on the site of a 1375 manor house. Take a walk inside the large courtyard—

PLACE DU MARCHÉ STE. CATHERINE

SQUARE CHARLES VICTOR LANGLOIS

PLACE VOSGES

HOTEL DE SULLY

HOTEL DE CLISSON

ARCHIVES NATIONALE

FONTAINE HAUDRIETTES

MUSEE DE L' HISTOIRE DE FRANCE

ARCHIVES NATIONALE

RUE DES ARCHIVES

Rendez-vous des Amis

cour d'honneur—even if you aren't up for a museum visit. **Archives Nationale** was set up in 1796 to retrieve and protect both state and private documents, some of which had been seized in the Revolution. This branch covers a period before 1958—way before, since it includes a 625 AD papyrus document from the Abbey of St. Denis, as well as dozens of records from the reign of Charlemagne circa 800 AD. The archive's bookshelves, placed end-to-end, would stretch more than 60 miles.

Despite its ambitious name, **Musee de l'Historie de France** is small enough for a quick stop and sees relatively few visitors. You are free to roam the former royal living quarters, with their 25-foot ceilings, gilded wall panels, and plush draperies. An admission is charged. Fireplaces and mirrors line the rococo-style rooms, including the stylish Salon Ovale. Clocks tick as if the princess were due back at any minute. Adjacent to Soubise is **Hotel de Rohan**, which is accessible at #87 Rue Vieille du Temple. Now part of the Archives Nationale, the building is named for the three Cardinals de Rohan who lived here in succession beginning in 1704.

EXIT THE ARCHIVES AND GO RIGHT AT THE CORNER, ON RUE DES ARCHIVES AND CONTINUE FOR SEVERAL BLOCKS TO THE CROSS STREET OF RUE DE BRETAGNE.

A stroll along **Rue de Braque** (go left from Rue des Archives after one block) will reveal examples of stately 17C residences. When crossing Rue des Quatre Fils, look left on the corner across Rue des Archives to see **Fontaine Haudriettes**, built in 1764 to replace an earlier version that had been distributing water around the arrondissement for a century. At #60 Rue des Archives is **Musee de la Chasse (Hunting) et de Nature** which was given a complete makeover in 2007. The exhaustive, if somewhat musty, historic collection of a French industrialist is now artfully displayed in the mid-17C **Hotel de Guenegaud**. You'll find a stash of daggers, crossbows, powder flasks, swords, and the like, along with unexpectedly thoughtful representations of the various animals and their importance in the symbology of medieval life in Europe. The new inventive decor sets off the collections. Guenegaud was designed by the influential architect **Francois Mansart** (1655), and is one the best remaining examples of his work.

At #58 is **Hotel de Clisson**. The turrets and gate are remnants (restored in part) of the 1380 mansion, which passed from its namesake through centuries of other prominent owners until becoming part of the National Archives. Bookstores and cafes encourage dawdling in this neighborhood.

AT RUE DE BRETAGNE, VEER LEFT ACROSS THE STREET INTO SQUARE DU TEMPLE.

Locals retreat from a busy neighborhood to the park benches in **Square du Temple**, which is one of 24 such parks laid out by **Baron Haussmann** in the vast city plan enacted during the Second Empire under Napoleon III. Ten years later, in 1867, design genius **Jean Charles Alphand** transformed the square into an English-garden style, adding more than 300 exotic plants and trees, and bringing rocks from Fontainebleau to create a cascade with pond. The garden gate is by **Davioud**, designer of Fontaine St. Michel.

The serene setting belies Square du Temple's infamous past. Beginning in the 13C the site was a feudal stronghold of the **Knights of Templar**, who controlled lands from here to Place de Republique.

A 16C monastery with an imposing **tower and fortress** became a prison during the Revolution for French royals—including Louis XVI, Marie Antoinette, and their son, the Dauphin, who disappeared mysteriously. The structures, with walls four-feet thick, were demolished on order of Emperor Napoleon in 1811.

DOUBLE-BACK TO RUE DE BRETAGNE AND GO LEFT. PASS RUELLE SOURDIS DE BEAUCE.

With delectables to delight foodies and a small garden in support of today's grow-where-you-live trend, **Le Marche Enfants Rouge** seems contemporary. But it is the oldest still-active food market in Paris, built in 1615 under Louis XIII. Its intriguing name derives from an orphanage from back then, where the children wore red uniforms.

Both fresh and prepared foods are sold in the enclosed market, which manages to fit in tables made cheery under light from a glass-and-wrought-iron ceiling. Organic produce and fresh flowers are worthy of a portrait. Standard French cheeses, crepes, seafood, and meats are balanced by a range of ethnic fare (Asian, Moroccan, Cajun, Italian). Locals hang here amid a convivial atmosphere, and the few tourists who wander in are welcomed.

DOUBLE BACK TO RUELLE SOURDIS DE BEAUCE AND GO LEFT. IN A SERIES OF SHORT BLOCKS: GO LEFT ON NARROW RUE PASTOURELLE, RIGHT ON RUE CHARLOT, AND LEFT AGAIN ON RUE DU PERCHE. AFTER A SHORT BLOCK, CROSS RUE VIEILLE DU TEMPLE, JOG RIGHT AND GO LEFT ON RUE DES COUTURES ST. GERVAIS.

This zigzag through narrow streets takes you past 14C enclaves, alongside numerous 21C concept boutiques and independent galleries. Narrow **Rue Pastourelle** is named after a leader in the French Parliament in 1378. **Rue Charlot** is thought by some to be the most with-it fashionista zone in the Marais, if not Paris, hinged around the recent renovation of the 17C **Hotel de Retz**. Hip fashion gives way to art galleries on **Rue Perche** and **Rue des Coutures St. Gervais**. The quarter is not flashy, but keen eyes will spot galleries well known to the global art market, as well as up-and-comer ventures.

AT THE END OF GERVAIS, GO RIGHT ON RUE DE THORIGNY AND CONTINUE TO THE END OF THE BLOCK.

At 5 Rue de Thorigny is **Musee Picasso**, a life-spanning repository of works by one of the most influential people of the twentieth century. Not long before his death in 1973, the artist proclaimed, "I am the greatest collector of Picassos in the world," a truth that came in handy when the French government acquired the art in lieu inheritance taxes. Taxes also built the 17C mansion, in which the collection is grandly presented, **Hotel Sale**. "Hotel Salt" is a cheeky reference to "Old Salty," a.k.a., Aubert de Fontenay, the man who made a fortune off a tax on salt for Louis XIV, until a financial scandal caused him to lose his home and office in disgrace.

A grandiose ironwork staircase from a courtyard provides a fitting entrée to **Musee Picasso's** 200-plus paintings and 150 sculpted pieces, plus drawings and sketches. Also displayed are works by Cezanne, Matisse, Degas, and other paintings collected by Picasso. An admission is charged. Throughout the museum the artworks are complimented by the artful decorations of the building itself—which recently received the

SQUARE LEOPOLD ACHILLE

RUE DE SÉVIGNÉ

4ᵉ ARR·

4ᵉ ARR·
RUE DES FRANCS BOURGEOIS

21 · 23 · PÂT

LE MARCHE ENFANTS ROUGE

MUSEE PICASSO

modern touch of a major renovation. All of Pablo Picasso's periods are represented beginning with his arrival in Paris at age 23, although the works from 1920s and 30s are most prevalent. Visitors may leave unsure of the nuances of the "blue period" versus the "pink period," and so forth, but for most an over-arching sense of the man's genius will linger.

FROM MUSEE PICASSO, CONTINUE DOWN THORIGNY A SHORT DISTANCE AND CURVE LEFT ON RUE DU PARC ROYAL. AFTER THE PARK, TURN RIGHT ON RUE DE SEVIGNE.

The little park on the right before Sevigne, **Square Leopold Achille**, and the similar one behind it on Rue Payenne, **Square Georges Cain**, both are circa 1900s. But both have roots in the 14C, as an extension of gardens when kings of France resided nearby in the former **Hotel Tournelles** (torn down to build Place Vosges). Mothers and au pairs with high-society kids in tow still refer to the squares as the "Royal Park." If you sit for a rest among exotic plantings (Siberian elm, Japanese holly) at the square, don't forget to admire the stately 17C mansions on its perimeter.

The most celebrated building in the quarter, at #23 Rue de Sevigne, is **Hotel de Carnavalet**, built in 1548 for the president of the French parliament, but best known as the 20-year residence of **Madame Sevigne** (1626-1696), the granddame of the Marais. The aristocratic Sevigne was widowed when her husband lost a duel over a mistress at age 26, and never remarried. She wrote a series of pithy and insightful letters to her daughter and others over a 30-year span, which have become a de facto history of the era in the Marais.

The classical Renaissance mansion was purchased by the government in 1866 to store artifacts recovered from buildings being dismantled by Haussmann's re-do of the entire city. The enterprise has evolved to become **Musee de l'Historie de Paris-Carnavalet**—a museum devoted to the history of Paris. Ambitious displays range from dugout canoes of the pre-Roman Gallic Parisii tribe before the first century, to a Belle Époque bedroom recreation of Marcel Proust, in which he wrote a novel based in part on Madame Sevigne's chronicles.

You'll find dioramas showing the Ile de la Cite in 1527 and the Bastille before the Revolution. A scale model of the guillotine is not far from the chess pieces Louis XVI used while waiting for a date with a real one. Entire rooms were moved here from Place des Vosges mansions. The entire museum is arranged sort of chronologically. Exhibits are interspersed with artifacts, like chunks of the original Hotel de Ville, the Nazareth archway from the Palais de la Cite, and other remnants otherwise lost in time. Creaky parquet floors lead to grand staircases and open onto a formal garden in the courtyard.

FROM SEVIGNE, GO LEFT ON RUE DES FRANCS BOURGEOIS. THEN GO RIGHT ON RUE DE TURENNE (REVISITING A SHORT BLOCK YOU DID EARLIER IN THE TOUR) AND CONTINUE TO BUSY RUE ST. ANTOINE. CROSS AND CONTINUE STRAIGHT ON RUE ST. PAUL.

To your right, after crossing Rue St. Antoine, is **Passage St. Paul**, providing a side entrance to the imposing **St. Paul-St. Louis**, an Italian-inspired church built by the Jesuits in 1641 on land donated by Louis XIII. Though restored in the 19C, the building retains a brooding Gothic aura. Original glass-and-floral friezes under a central dome are lofted 160-feet above. Delacroix's Christ in the Garden evokes the

MUSEE CARNAVALET

SUN KING, MUSEE CARNAVALET

SQUARE GEORGES CAIN

religious solemnity of the vast space. The church was sited on one of four entrances to Paris along the Philippe Auguste wall. Double back to Rue St. Paul, where at #32 is a fragment of the belfry of a chapel dismantled in 1350.

FROM RUE ST. PAUL, GO RIGHT ON RUE CHARLEMAGNE.

As you walk behind the church St. Paul-St. Louis, look for an opening on your left to **Village St. Paul**—an enclave of cobblestone courtyards with about 200 antique dealers. These former gardens and official residences of King Charles V had all the inconveniences of their 14C heritage until given a modern overhaul, which began in 1970 and lasted for a decade. True heirlooms are available for sale and it's okay to bargain. Wander around to find paintings, glassware, antique dolls, rustic farm tools, vintage dresses, and crafts boutiques—but try to exit the same way you came in. If hunger strikes make your way to #7, Cru (raw), a cool modern restaurant featuring salads, tartares, carpaccios served with a twist.

CONTINUE ON RUE CHARLEMAGNE AND THEN GO LEFT ON CURVING RUE FIGUIER.

On Rue Charlemagne is the largest remaining segment of the **Philippe Auguste wall**, which was a three-plus mile fortification built by the king at the turn of the 12C to protect Paris from the Normans while he embarked on the Crusades. Now integrated into other buildings, this section contains one of the wall's 77 guard towers, which were arranged about 60 feet apart, a distance set within range of the weapons of the day. Its height ranged from 20 to 25 feet, made taller by wooden embattlements along the top in places.

AT THE SHARP CORNER, GO RIGHT ON RUE DE L' HOTEL DE VILLE.

Hotel de Sens is one of the city's two remaining Gothic residences complete with watchtower and dungeon (the other being Hotel Cluny on the Left Bank that is now an acclaimed museum for the Middle Ages). Critics complain about the authenticity of renovations made after the city purchased the building in 1911, but the end results have captured the vision of what a storybook castle should look like. Much of the original archecture remains. It is now a reference library for the decorative fine arts—with a reading room open to the public.

Hotel de Sens had a long lists of tenants after being built for Tristan de Salazar, the Archbishop of Sens. The most notorious was **Queen Margot**—La Reine Margot, or Marguerite de Valois. The daughter of Henry II, she became the ex-wife of Henry IV and took up residence here in 1605 to live out her last ten years. She was romantically voracious, taking on lovers well into her 50s, and, since she was balding, was said to make wigs from her paramours' hair.

In 1606, a spurned flame killed a new lover, and then the queen watched from a window as the second lover, the Count of Vermont, was beheaded in the street. Even with all that, Queen Margot is best known as a key figure in the religious-political machinations of the time. Her memoirs, published posthumously, were the basis of an 1845 novel by Alexandre Dumas, and two movies, the last highly acclaimed in 1995, *Queen Margot*, starring Isabelle Adjani.

HOTEL DE SENS

END AT PONT MARIE STOP, LINE 7. IT'S LOCATED ON RUE HOTEL DE VILLE.

RUE DE LAPPE

WALKING TOUR SEVEN

POSTCARD PLACES:

Place de la Bastille ... Bassin de l'Arsenal ... Viaduc des Arts ... Promenade Plantee ... Place d'Aligre ... Rue Faubourg-St. Antoine ... Rue de Lappe ... Opera de Paris Bastille

THUMBNAIL:

Pick a weekend morning to walk or jog along paths of historical significance—beside a yacht harbor and on a miles-long elevated greenway. Then get lost in a huge old-world market square and flea market. Pick any evening for Parisian cabaret and cafe life, circa 21C. The new opera house gleams at Place de la Bastille, site of the obelisk that symbolizes where the French Revolution finally took to the streets.

BIG PICTURE:

Though of interest to all, Walking Tour Seven will probably open new doors for repeat visitors to Paris. This hip-and-cool *quartier* sees fewer tourists, though it hums with locals.

DISTANCE: 1.5 to 2.75 miles   TIME: 2.5 to 4.5 hours

Place de la Bastille

BASSIN DE L'ARSENAL

BELOW PROMENADE PLANTÉE

RUE DE LAPPE

MARCHÉ D'ALIGRE

PROMENADE PLANTÉE

PASSAGE DU CHANTIER

SQUARE TROUSSEAU

WALKING TOUR
Seven

START AT THE BASTILLE METRO STOP, LINES 1, 8, AND 10.

WITH PLACE DE LA BASTILLE (WHICH YOU WILL REVISIT) AT YOUR BACK, WALK DOWN BLVD. DE LA BASTILLE (NEW BASTILLE OPERA WILL BE ON YOUR LEFT BUT DON'T WALK DOWN RUE DE LYON BY MISTAKE). THEN HEAD RIGHT DOWN A COBBLESTONE RAMP.

In the 19C, **Bassin de Arsenal** was connected to Canal St. Martin, a waterway that moved the manufacturing commerce of Faubourg-St. Antoine to the Seine. Before that, portions of the basin were the moat for the prison at Bastille. Today, a controlled lock and nearly 200 moorings make it ideal for leisure craft and exercise walkers. You may wish to take a look from the footbridge. You may also walk farther down the marina to where it joins the Seine at Port de Plaisance, but then double back as directed below.

JUST PAST THE FOOTBRIDGE, GO LEFT ON RUE JULES CESAR. CROSS RUE DE LYON AND AVE. DAUMESNIL AND HEAD TOWARD BRICK ARCHWAYS. GO UP STAIRS AND WALK RIGHT ON THE ELEVATED WALKWAY. NOTE: YOU WILL PASS THE WALK'S EXIT AND DOUBLE BACK ON THE PROMENADE. READ THE NEXT DIRECTIONS TO DETERMINE THE EXIT POINT, IF YOU WISH TO SHORTEN THE WALK.

The remains of a freight railway borders Rue Daumesnil, elevated on a viaduct comprised of a series of brick arches. It was used to haul goods to the periphery of Paris for a century, until the line was abandoned in 1959. Rather than tear the antiquated line down in 2000, they've turned it into the city's longest and skinniest park—**Promenade Plantee**. For more than a mile, a profusion of rose bushes, lavender, bamboo, and flowerbeds border the paved-and-decked pathway,

sometimes under the shade of cherry and maples trees, sometimes revealing cityscapes. Of particular note are the 12 reproductions of Michelangelo's *The Dying Slave* that top the arrondissement's police station.

At one section is a long narrow pond, bracketed by trellises. The promenade becomes a stainless-steel-and-wooden span at **Jardin de Reuilly**. Apartment dwellers sprawl on the park's lawn, rising perhaps to sip la petillante ("the bubbly"), which is free sparking water dispensed from a fountain provided by Eau de Paris in an effort to wean Parisians from plastic water bottles. Reuilly, a park since 1994, is on the site of a former chateau of the Merovingian Kings of the first century. The path continues to Bois Vincennes, but you will probably want to turn around and go back to the spot indicated in the next directions paragraph below.

Directly below the promenade is the **Viaduc des Arts**, some 50 glass-façaded shops occupying many of the 70-plus brick archways of the former railway track. Many of the most accomplished artisans in Paris put their skills and artwork on display. Taken as a whole, the shops perpetuate the cultural and professional heritage of this *quartier*, the Faubourg-Saint-Antoine, known historically as a birthplace of artistic styles. Stairways lead down to the shops.

AT A SMALL PARK WITH ELEVATOR (LESS THAN A HALF-MILE ALONG THE PROMENADE) GO DOWN TO STREET LEVEL (RUE HECTOR MALOT). AT THE NEXT BLOCK, GO LEFT ON RUE DE CHARENTON AND THEN IMMEDIATELY RIGHT ON RUE D'ALIGRE.

Marche d'Aligre, located at the place of the same name, is the cheapest and perhaps liveliest market street in Paris

VIADUC DES ARTS

MARCHÉ BEAUVAU

PLACE D'ALIGRE

to buy the wide range of all things edible from the **Ile de France**—brokered by North African and Arab vendors proud to shout the quality of their goods. Weekends are best, when the narrow street is jammed early in the day. The market is closed Mondays. Apartments ring the **Place d'Aligre**, which was renovated in 2005 and is the site of flea markets and art fairs. Although the sidewalks of Rue d'Aligre are laden with an abundance of colorful produce, the market's focus is the 18C pavilion, **Marche Beauvau**. A truss-beam ceiling provides plenty of open space around a central fountain and is filled with displays of cheeses, flowers, seafood and shellfish, meats and sausages, herbs, fruits, and produce—from Provence, Limousin, Charlais, and other provinces of France.

PAST THE PLACE, VEER LEFT ON RUE CROZATIER FOR A SHORT DISTANCE TO RUE DU FAUBOURG SAINT ANTOINE. GO LEFT TWO SHORT BLOCKS. CROSS THE STREET AND DOUBLE BACK ON SAINT ANTOINE.

Rue Faubourg Saint Antoine historically was the only road east through the swamps from Paris. It was the domain of cabinetmakers and craftsmen, plying their trade in the passages and narrow streets of the quarter. On your left is **Square Trousseau**, a pleasant neighborhood park enjoyed mainly by children, and weary tourists—but more widely associated with the bistro of the same name on the corner that is frequented by arty media types. Regular patrons include fashion designer Jean Paul Gaultier (a protégé of Pierre Cardin who has created his own empire) and original super model, Claudia Schiffer.

Across Rue Faubourg Saint Antoine from the square is **Cour du Saint Esprit**, home to local artists. To the left of the court is

Passage de la Bonne Graine (Good Seed), a name made famous in a 1946 song by **Edith Piaf**. The passage is a locale for design and acting workshops, as well as organic restaurants.

GO BACK ON RUE DE FAUBOURG SAINT ANTOINE AND PASS RUE TROUSSEAU. THEN GO LEFT ON PASSAGE ST. BERNARD. GO LEFT AGAIN AT THE FIRST SMALL STREET, RUE DE CANDLE (WHICH BECOMES RUE DE LA MAIN D'OR) AND THEN GO RIGHT ON PASSAGE DE LA MAIN D'OR. CROSS RUE DE CHARONNE, JOG RIGHT, AND THEN GO LEFT ON PASSAGE CHARLES DALLERY.

Passage St. Bernard is encased by sleek apartments of Italian design, a distinctly modern redevelopment in one of the more densely populated neighborhoods in Europe. Small galleries, jazz cafes, and artful graffiti reveal the demographic of the area. At #15 **Passage de la Main d'Or** is the offbeat theatre that draws most visitors to the quarter. Quieter apartments with flowerpots on balconies and birds flitting about mark **Passage Charles Dallery**.

CROSS AVE. LEDRU ROLLIN AND IMMEDIATELY GO LEFT ON PASSAGE BULLOURDE AND THEN RIGHT ON RUE KELLER. WALK LEFT AT RUE DE LA ROQUETTE. CONTINUE TO RUE LAPPE, AND GO LEFT AGAIN.

The next few turns of the tour are through the neighborhoods of young artists, entrepreneurs, techie designers, club-goers, and offbeat urbanites. This new generation continues a tradition of social liveliness that began during the French Revolution, scorched right on through the Roaring 20s, and became the heart of the French Liberation. Narrow **Passage Bullourde** has some coveted, downscale work-live apartments mixed in with vacation rentals, though the atmosphere is made homier in the daytime by a large school. In recent years on **Rue Keller**, a critical mass of the talented and trendy have opened Bohemian shops, avant-garde boutiques, quasi-kinky galleries to create a sum greater than the parts—and a magnet for more of the fashion intelligencia to move into more lofts. Here, the basic-black of chic gives way to candy-cane pink. Bars are hopping at happy hour. Among a string of galleries on Rue Keller, look for Anne Willi at #13, Gaelle Barre at #17, and Moloko across the street at #18.

The restaurants and bistros amplify on **Rue de la Roquette**. But in the 17C, Roquette was but a rural road leading to the large domain of a convent of the same name—which derives from a pale yellow flower, "the rocket," that thrived in the rubble beside the road. At the time of the Revolution and for a century thereafter, Roquette was known as the "Sinister Way," or "Sorrowful Road." It connected the prison at Bastille to the new cemetery at Pere Lachaise, passing two other prisons, both a men's and women's. Funerals and bawdy public executions by guillotine were frequent. To your right as you reach the Roquette, at #76, is **Theatre de La Bastille**, where the quarter's new vibe is apparent in dance and drama performances that warp and create trends.

For all its vibrancy, the scene on Roquette is but prelude to the action of **Rue Lappe**. Wrought-iron balconies speak of the street's heritage of ironworkers and artisans. On July 17, 1789, these working stiffs of the emerging Third Estate joined with other craftsmen, merchants, and radicals of the working class and met at **Cour St. Louis** (on your right, midway down Rue Lappe). Later that night they "stormed the Bastille," thus beginning the Revolution. Their group was called Sans Culottes, a rejection of the fashionable knickers worn by the aristocratic men. At #27 is the **Bistro les Sans Culottes**, although this meeting place got started in the 1920s as a watering hole for absinthe drinkers. Dancehall music with accordion bands —**bal musette**—got its boost on Rue Lappe, owing to the heritage of people of Auvergne who moved in. At #6 is **Aux Produits d'Auvergne**, a century-old market that was recently spared closing by neighborhood petition. In the 1930s there were some 20 bars and dancehalls, the most famous at #9 **Balajo**. This club was where torch singer Edith Pilaf wowed a packed house and Marlene Dietrich was among the celebrity regulars. The bawdy, seedy atmosphere caused writers like Henry Miller to wax romantic. After the French Liberation of WWII, celebrations along Rue Lappe were epic.

FROM THE END OF RUE LAPPE, GO RIGHT ON RUE DE CHARONNE. THEN CROSS RUE DU FAUBOURG ST. ANTOINE AND GO STRAIGHT INTO PASSAGE DU CHANTIER. THEN GO RIGHT ON RUE DE CHARENTON TO PLACE DE LA BASTILLE.

No cobblestone alley in Paris is more of a time machine to the 18C than **Passage du Chantier**. Cubbyhole furniture shops, like le Manor de Gilles, have been there for generations, and if Louis XVI needed repairs or new chairs for the salon, these artisans could set him up. An undulating walkway and apartments that span overhead between stone walls make this passage particularly picturesque.

A block up Rue de Charenton, modernity sparkles abruptly into focus at the **Opera de Paris Bastille**, a curving four-block wall of glass, steel, and white granite. It opened in 1989 on the 200th anniversary

Passage St. Bernard

Rue de la Roquette

41

à GALOCHE d'BURILLAC

RESTAURANT AUVERGNAT

Rue Keller

Rue de Lappe

BISTROT LES SANS CULOTTES

DE LA MAIN D'OR

L'Opera de Paris Bastille

SIDDHARTA
PREL JOCA /
MANTOVANI / LÉVÊQUE

of the storming of the Bastille. The project was 20 years in the making, which also motivated the groovy renaissance for the entire quarter. Architect Carlos Ott's design was the chosen one from among 750 plans submitted at the behest of President Francois Mitterrand. The opera's 2,700-plus black-velvet seats are only about 500 more than the Opera Garnier that it replaced. But the auditorium is less than five percent of the opera building's total cubic space: There are ten stories underground, and an enormous backstage allows for entire sets to be wheeled on and off intact.

A lively sidewalk scene is guaranteed at **Place de la Bastille**, but the only reminder of the infamous prison is a 160-foot bronze column, the **Colonne de Juilliet**. The spire was erected 31 years after the Revolution, to commemorate the Revolution of 1830—when the reign of Charles X ended and the advent of France's "citizen-king" Louis-Philippe began. Names of the some 500 people who died in the revolution are etched in the bronze. Atop the column is a 16-foot gilded figure, "The Spirit of Freedom," looking sprite, balanced on one foot, winged, and holding a torch. Hundreds of people are buried beneath the column, from the 1830 revolution and from yet another uprising in 1848.

Bastille a Porte San Antoine in 1370 was a fortress with eight, 100-foot towers at a gate in the city wall. Bastille provided a safe royal residence for Charles V. Paris expanded beyond this gate over the centuries, and Bastille was converted to a prison by Cardinal Richelieu in the 17C. Under Louis XIII, Bastille held political undesirables, though it did not have the reputation as a horror chamber like other French prisons. **Voltaire** did a stint here as a result of his satire. A "heretic" clergyman was allowed to have 20 people in as dinner guests. "The Man in the Iron Mask," was imprisoned for witchcraft. **Marquis de Sade** had a cell here before being shipped to an insane asylum just 10 days before the storming of the Bastille. Still, the brooding mass of stone was a symbol of despotism, of a time when irritating someone important resulted in imprisonment. Only six prisoners were freed as the Revolution began, costing the lives of 100 revolutionaries.

END AT THE BASTILLE METRO STOP, LINES 1, 8, AND 10.

BASTILLE METRO

BASTILLE

COLONNE DE JUILLET

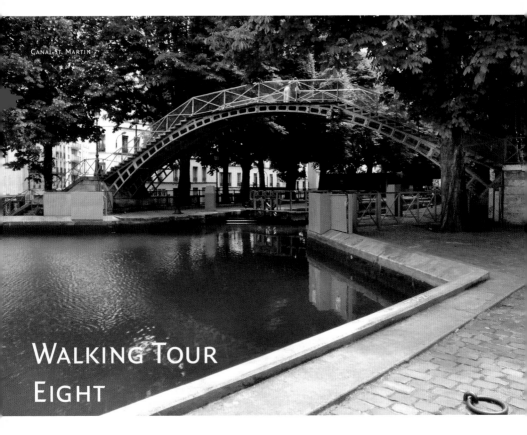

CANAL ST. MARTIN

WALKING TOUR
EIGHT

POSTCARDS:

Place de Rhin et Danube ... Villas Quartier Mouzaia ... Parc des Buttes Chaumont ... Canal Saint Martin ... Hotel du Nord ... Hopital Saint Louis ... Promenade Richard Lenoir ... Place de la Republique

THUMBNAIL:

This quaint village feels removed to the French countryside. From here, the paths of Buttes Chaumont, with its small lake and bridges, wind down to the photogenic footbridges of Canal St. Martin. The dreamy cityscape comes to an end at Place de la Republique, the memorial to the revolution—and today the site of regular political demonstrations.

BIG PICTURE:

Walking Tour Eight is a stroll, with park benches that invite a *reposer*. To make this an all-day outing, with variety, start with this walk and then continue to Walking Tour Six— joining it at Square du Temple. The longer walk is all downhill to the Seine.

DISTANCE: 2.75 to 4 miles   TIME: 3.5 to 5 hours

ANTOINE ET LILI

CANAL ST. MARTIN

PARC DE BUTTES CHAUMONT

PLACE DE LA REPUBLIQUE

QUAI DE VALMY

CANAL ST. MARTIN

Quartier Mouzaia villas

WALKING TOUR
Eight

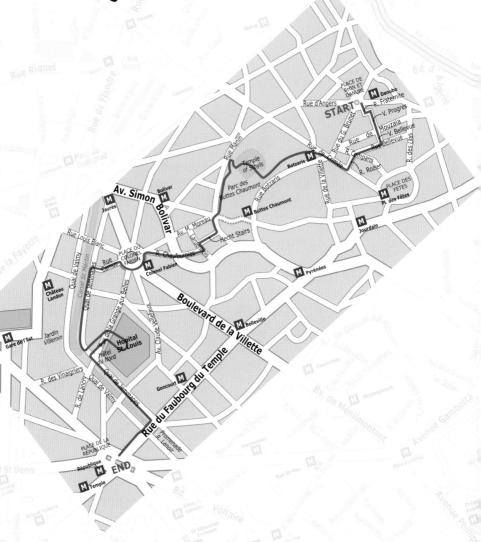

START AT THE DANUBE METRO STOP, LINE 7B.

FROM THE DANUBE METRO, EXIT TO PLACE DE RHIN ET DANUBE, A HILLSIDE WHERE SEVEN STREETS CONVERGE. VEER RIGHT, AND UPHILL ON SMALLER RUE DE LA FRATERNITE. THEN JOG LEFT ON RUE DE L'EGALITE, AND THEN GO RIGHT, UPHILL ON VILLA DU PROGRES. CROSS RUE DE MOUZAIA AND CONTINUE STRAIGHT ON VILLA DU BELLEVUE.

Emerging from the metro at **Place de Rhin et Danube**, you may wonder if you missed a stop or three and wound up in the country a hundred miles from Paris. Seven streets join on a quiet hilltop.

Go south on a slight ascent on Rue de la Fraternite to begin a tour of **Quartier Mouzaia**—some 20 cobblestone alleyways alongside the courtyards of rustic brick, stucco and wood bungalows. Most cottages have colorful gardens, and greenery overhangs much of the route. The neighborhood, most of which branches off Rue Mouzaia, was built over twenty years around the turn of the 20C as a worker's subdivision, though it's a far cry from the uniformity that word evokes. Reaching the top of **Villa du Bellevue**, you may wish to go left on Rue du Bellevue to see several more villas before continuing.

AT THE TOP OF VILLA BELLEVUE, GO RIGHT ON RUE DU BELLEVUE AND THEN RIGHT AGAIN ON RUE COMPANS. THEN JOG LEFT ON RUE ARTHUR ROZIER AND THEN GO RIGHT DOWN STAIRS AT VILLA ALBERT ROBIDA. AT THE BOTTOM, CROSS RUE DE CRIMEE AND GO RIGHT TO THE CORNER. ENTER PARC DES BUTTES CHAUMONT.

Parc des Buttes Chaumont, 60 sylvan acres on the upslope of Paris, may seem like a setting for a tryst in a period novel, but its history is far from romantic. In the 13C its ravines were used as a refuse dump, where the bodies of livestock were dumped and despicable criminals were displayed in an iron cage called a "gibbet." During the Renaissance the site was a dreary, scarred gypsum (plaster of Paris) quarry, providing materials for architectural decorations and facades. During the Belle Époque, Napoleon III had enough of the eyesore, and ordered Paris's modern planners Baron Haussmann and Jean Charles Alphand to transform it into a park. With the help of dynamite and 1,000 workers, the job was completed over a four-year span, ending in 1867.

Enter **Parc de Buttes Chaumont** and keep left on a treed path that attracts joggers. There are many interconnected trails, but you'll probably want to stay high, passing the Rosa Bonheur restaurant. Then drop down past a cascade to a footbridge, **Pont des Suicides**, which leads to the **Temple of Sibyls**, a small classical colonnaded kiosk perched atop **Belvedere Island** in the park's small lake. The temple affords views, near and far. Leave the island a different way, westerly, across a stainless-steel railed suspension footbridge. To see other park features—a grotto with swans and waterfowl, the music kiosk, and marionette theater—go right from the footbridge to explore a lakeside path. Then double back—left from the steel bridge—and follow a main path past the **Pavillon du Lac**, a restaurant as old as the park. Continue to the park exit on Rue Manin, across from Avenue Mathurin Moreau.

EXIT PARC BUTTES CHAUMONT, CROSS RUE MANIN AND GO LEFT. AT RUE PHILIPPE HECHT, GO RIGHT UP THE FLIGHTS OF STAIRS, AND CONTINUE ON COBBLESTONE STREET. GO LEFT ON CURVING RUE GEORGES LARDENNOIS AND THEN GO RIGHT ON A FOOTPATH THROUGH A NEIGHBORHOOD

TEMPLE OF SIBYLS

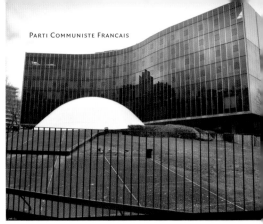

PARTI COMMUNISTE FRANCAIS

QUARTIER MOUZAÏA

PLACE DE RHIN ET DANUBE

GREENSPACE. AT THE BOTTOM GO STRAIGHT ON RUE DES CHAUFOURNIERS AND THEN LEFT ON RUE MATHURIN MOREAU TO PLACE DU COLONEL FABIEN.

The staircases of **Rue Philippe Hecht** lead to a village-like neighborhood and then to long views, most notably of the church of Sacre Coeur lofted above the right bank. After dropping through the small park, you'll reach **Rue des Chaufourniers,** a street named for the large ovens that were used to cure the gypsum from the quarry at Buttes Chaumont. (If the park path is closed, double back on Rue Lardennois and continue down to Avenue Moreau.)

The eight-street roundabout at **Place du Colonel Fabien** is best known as the location of the futuristic headquarters for the **Parti Communiste Francais (PCF)**. The big white bubble rising from the garden is the roof of the building's subterranean auditorium. Colonel Fabien was the nom-de-guerre of **Pierre Georges**, a communist member of the Resistance who assassinated the first Germans in Paris during the war. He himself was killed in 1944, and the place was named in his honor a year later.

GO AROUND LEFT ON PLACE FABIEN AND TAKE SMALL RUE ALBERT CAMUS (STRAIGHT ACROSS FROM MOREAU). CONTINUE ON THE BRICK WALKWAY AND THROUGH A SMALL PARK ON RUE HAENDEL. REACH CANAL ST. MARTIN AND GO LEFT ALONG THE QUAI DE JEMMAPES.

The brick courtyard of **Rue Albert Camus** leads to **Place Robert Desnos** (a surrealist poet killed during WWII) and connects with the park at **Rue G.F. Haendel**—all of this a pedestrian corridor encased by apartments. The route opens up to **Canal St. Martin.**

In 1802, Emperor Napoleon ordered the digging of **Canal St. Martin**, a waterway to transport grain and other materials into the denser area of Paris, and to supply the fresh water needed to avoid dysentery, cholera, and other diseases. Some 23 years later, the 3-mile project was completed. Today the series of curving bridges and nine locks (allowing vessels to rise and fall 80 feet) are parkland for pedestrians.

Auto traffic is prohibited on Sundays, when peds and bikes rule the streets. Leafy chestnut trees and gardens shade squares on both sides of the canal. Cross **Quai de Jemmapes** to see one of the locks, and then go left down the canal—which gets more picturesque as you proceed. Across the canal, where it makes a bend, is **Jardin Villemin**, a five-acre neighborhood park. And past the park is the beginning of the so-cool boutiques and galleries along the canal. At #93 Quai de Valmy is **Sando**, and next door (look for the Lifesaver colors) is **Antoine & Lili**, part of a chain, filled with quirky, girly originals. On this side of the canal, at #102 Quai de Jemmapes, is **Hotel du Nord**, which was renovated in the 1990s, thus initiating the gentrification of the quartier. A 1938 film by Marcel Carne, with the hotel as its title, is a fatalistic noir classic about star-crossed lovers.

AT THE SECOND ARCHED BRIDGE, GO LEFT ON RUE DE LA GRANGE AUX BELLES. PASS RUE BICHAT AND THEN GO RIGHT INTO THE ENTRANCE OF HOPITAL SAINT LOUIS. NOTE: ANOTHER ENTRANCE, ON RUE BICHAT ACROSS FROM AVENUE RICHERAND, IS CLOSED ON WEEKENDS.

Though **Hopital Saint Louis** is now a modern facility, the walk through the short tunnel into the courtyard is a trip back to the early 17C. Henry IV had the hospital built to house victims of the plague. The

as **Promenade Richard Lenoir**—with flowered water gardens and tree-lined paths that enfold all the way to Place de la Bastille, where the water surfaces again as Bassin de Arsenal. **Napoleon III** wasn't looking to beautify the city when he ordered Haussmann to cover the lower section of the canal in the 1860s: The canal served as a moat defending the rebellious quarters of eastern Paris since the swinging bridges could be withdrawn to thwart the advance of government troops. Take a stroll down Lenoir, if you wish, then double back.

GO RIGHT ON RUE DE FAUBOURG DU TEMPLE TO PLACE DE LA REPUBLIQUE.

Seven major thoroughfares converge at the huge, rectangular **Place de la Republique**. The space was strategically created by Haussmann in 1854 to allow a quick response by the French Republican Guard, which is housed here at **Caserne Verines**. During the reign of Charles V in the late 14C, the area was the site of the Temple Gate in the wall that fortified Paris. In 1883, the current bronze statue of the allegorical female, **Marianne**, was erected, holding an olive branch to memorialize the virtues of the nation—Liberty, Equality, and Fraternity. The 30-foot high monument is complex in design. Brave the traffic to get close and admire the details. Among the decorations on the pedestal are a dozen stone bas-reliefs that depict the major political events taking place from 1789 to 1880. A bronze lion guards the scene. During today's demonstrations—the French still take their democracy to the streets—the entire memorial gets wallpapered with stickers.

site was normally downwind from Paris, and isolated by surrounding marshlands. Magnolias and stately leafy trees accent an inner square that is all about symmetry—a smaller version of Place des Vosges (see Walking Tour Six).

BACKTRACK TO CANAL ST. MARTIN, GO LEFT, AND CONTINUE TO RUE FAUBOURG DU TEMPLE.

You'll want to crisscross the remaining several bridges under the broadleaf trees of **Canal St. Martin** and nose around the many bistros and shops. It's surprising more romantic comedies haven't been shot here—though actress Audrey Tautou did skip stones in the canal during the final scenes of *Amelie*, France's top film of 2001. At Rue Faubourg du Temple, the canal goes underground, but the route continues

END AT REPUBLIQUE METRO STOP, LINES 3, 5, 8, 9, AND 11.

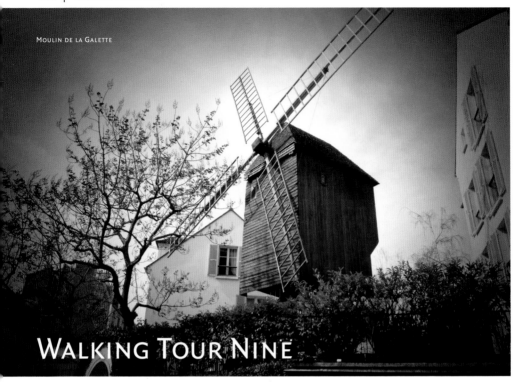

MOULIN DE LA GALETTE

WALKING TOUR NINE

POSTCARDS:

Moulin Rouge ... Rue Lepic ... Place Emile Goudeau ... Montmartre ... Sacre Coeur ... Place du Tertre ... Espace Salvador Dali ... Moulin de la Galette ... Square Suzanne Buisson ... Le Lapin Agile ... Parc de la Turlure ... Rue des Martyrs ... Notre Dame de Lorette

THUMBNAIL:

Religious shrines and churches have stood upon this hill above the swamplands of Paris since the first flickers of recorded history. Centuries later came the impoverished Impressionist painters (Van Gogh among them) to capture the light on canvas. Sacre Coeur, one of the symbols of Paris, is a recent addition. Winding streets rise from seedy Place Pigalle and the nearby nightclub Moulin Rouge, and swarms of tourists today create a carnival atmosphere. But Montmartre's cobblestones remain a gateway to quieter times.

BIG PICTURE:

This is an atmospheric walking tour, and you'll have plenty of time to get lost in a wonderful maze. Along with the Tour Eiffel and Notre Dame, Montmartre is one of the most-visited parts of Paris, inviting wall-to-wall souvenir shops and street performers. The lower boulevards hum with the activity of a working class neighborhood, an abrupt boundry to the tourist world.

DISTANCE: 3 to 4.5 miles   TIME: 2.5 to 4.5 hours

Rue Foyatier

Place de la Tertre

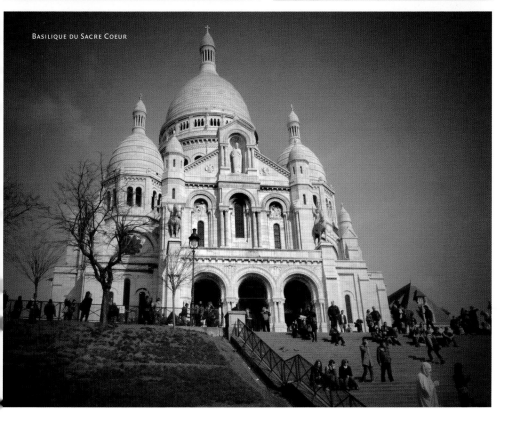
Basilique du Sacre Coeur

SQUARE SUZANNE BUISSON

RUE DE L'ABREUVOIR

NOTRE DAME DE LORETTE

WALKING TOUR
Nine

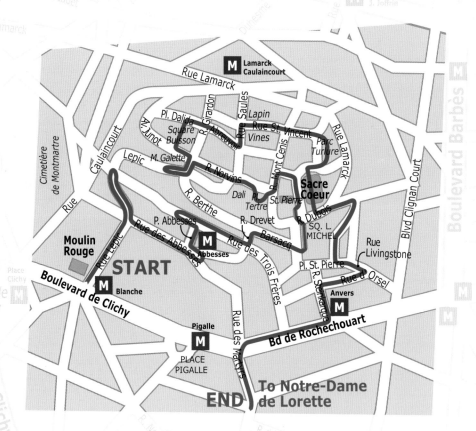

Boulevard Ney

Porte de
St Ouen

Rue Leibnitz

Porte de
Clignancourt

Rue Bellard

Rue Championnet

Rue Championnet

Rue Champion

Avenue de Sain

Boulevard Ornano

Guy
Moquet

Rue Marcadet

Rue Ordener

Simplon

J. Joffrin

Rue Lamarck

M Lamarck
Caulaincourt

Cimetière
de Montmartre

Rue Lamarck

Boulevard Barbès

Place de
Clichy

Place de
Clichy

Rue de Clichy

Rue de Clichy

Rue de Londres

Caulaincourt

Rue

Lepic

An. Junot

M. Galette

Pl. Dalida
Square
Buisson

R. Abreuvoir

Girardon

Saules

Lapin
Vines

Rue St. Vincent

Mont Cenis

Parc
Turlure

Rue Lamarck

Blvd Clignan Court

R. Norvins

R. Berthe

Dali
Pl.
Tertre

St. Pierre

Sacre
Coeur

P. Abbesses

R. Drevet

R. Dubois

SQ. L.
MICHEL

Rue
Livingstone

**Moulin
Rouge**

Rue Lepic

Rue des Abbesses

M

Abbesses

Barsacq

Rue des Trois Freres

Pl. St. Pierre

R. Steinkerque

Rue d'Orsel

Anvers

M

START

M Blanche

Boulevard de Clichy

Pigalle

M

PLACE
PIGALLE

Rue des Martyrs

Bd de Rochechouart

END

**To Notre-Dame
de Lorette**

R.a.l. Tour d'Auvergne

St Georges

Rue de Clichy

Rue Blanche

R. Notre Dame de Lorette

Rue des Martyrs

Place
d'Estienne
d'Orvers

Trinité

Rue de Châteaudun

Rue la Fayette

Cadet

Lazare

N. - D. de
Lorette

artin

Chaussée d'Antin

Le Peletier

START BLANCHE METRO STOP, LINE 2.

FROM PLACE BLANCHE WALK UP RUE LEPIC TO RUE ABBESSES.

The landmark at Place Blanche is the **Moulin Rouge**, a bawdy and provocative nightclub spinning like a windmill in a gale since it opened in 1889. The cancan, the leg-lifting, shrieking, twirling dance of the courtesans, started here before being toned down and spreading throughout Europe. In letters home, **William Faulkner** reported, "ladies come out clothed principally in lipstick," after he'd viewed a striptease—which also originated here. Posters by **Toulouse Lautrec** memorialize the early days at the Moulin Rouge, which has also been the title of six movies. Among the many stars to grace the stage have been Josephine Baker, Edith Piaf, Charles Aznavour, Frank Sinatra, Liza Minnelli, and Elton John.

Hope to be hungry ascending **Rue Lepic**, a street to appease a yen for anything edible. The lively neighborhood street is also a visual feast, with artfully displayed windows of patisseries, flower shops, and charcuteries. In 1809, **Napoleon** had difficulty climbing the steep street, so he had it rebuilt. But it is still steep: In 1898, Rue Lepic was the acid test for the car newly built by the **Renault brothers**, who won a bet by navigating the hill and then parlayed the winnings to start their company.

AT THE TOP, GO LEFT ON THE CONTINUATION OF RUE LEPIC. THEN DOUBLE BACK AND CONTINUE STRAIGHT ON RUE DES ABBESSES TO PLACE DES ABBESSES.

On your left at #33, as **Rue Lepic** begins its right curve, are the vine-covered walls of Le Baslic, an old-style French restaurant with exposed beams and smoke-stained chimney—though its prices are up to date. At #54 lived the street's most famous residents, **Vincent Van Gogh** and brother **Theo**, although they were hardly famous at the time in 1866. Vincent moved from here to the countryside, only to shoot himself years later, in 1890. Two months later Theo also committed suicide.

The art nouveau glass-roofed entry to the metro at **Place de Abbesses** by **Hector Guimard** was one of many he designed in the early 1900s, but only two remain. To catch a ride here, you'll need to go down about 300 steps. Surrounding the metro is **Square Jean Rictus**, a park where children play beside a large enameled mural that says, "I love you" in more than 300 languages. Across the street is **St. Jean de Montmartre**, a church whose red-brick façade covers Paris's first building of reinforced concrete, a new method that allowed for more room inside, but was greeted with skepticism and a lawsuit.

FACING PLACE DES ABBESSES, GO LEFT UP THE STAIRS OF PASSAGE DES ABESSES. AT THE TOP, GO LEFT ON RUE DES TROIS FERES.

Your first right off Rue des Trois Feres is Rue Ravignan, which leads to the unassuming **Place Emile Goudeau**—Montmartre's obscure-but-most-famous former enclave of painters and other artists. Its peak period was a decade on either side of 1900. In a studio here in 1905, **Picasso**, then 24, painted **Gertrude Stein**, who was 31. She traveled across Paris for some 90 sittings. Painter Max Jacob dubbed the falling-down assemblage of seedy shacks, **Bateau Lavoir**, the "wash house." Most of it burned down in 1970. Among others who worked here were Matisse, Braque, Utrillo, and Modigliani. By WWI, most artists exited Montmartre

Square Jean Rictus

Place de Abbesses

Rue La Vieuville

and moved to the Left Bank, near Montparnasse.

At #56 Rue des Trois Feres is **Aux Marche de la Butte**, a colorful display of fruits and flowers made more popular since being depicted as a favorite stop for Audrey Tautou in the film *Amelie*.

BACKTRACK ON RUE DES TROIS FERES. ACROSS FROM RUE LA VIEUVILLE, GO LEFT UP THE FLIGHTS OF STAIRS (WHICH IS RUE DREVET) TO RUE ANDRE BARSACQ. THEN GO RIGHT, DESCENDING PAST RUE CHAPPE TO THE LONG STAIRWAYS OF RUE FOYATIER. GO LEFT ON RUE FOYATIER AND CLIMB TO BASILIQUE DU SACRE COEUR.

The village cobblestones of Rue Barsacq give way to the multiple flights of stairs that march upward from the circus atmosphere of **Place Suzanne Valadon**— down on your right. Valadon was a painter and former mistress of Toulouse Lautrec. Street hucksters mix with photo-clicking tourists at the bottom, which is also the spot to queue up to ride the **Funiculare** car to the top (tickets costs one Euro or use a Metro ticket). Walkers will want to go left, following the lampposts up the eight or so tree-lined staircases of **Rue Foyatier**—built in 1867 and captured forever at the turn of the century in the evocative photographs by **Brassai**.

The climb gives way to Rue Cardinal Dubois, where two wide flights of stairs and a plaza (**Parvis Sacre Coeur**) provide a point-blank look at **Basilique du Sacre Coeur**, and serve as bleachers for throngs enjoying the view of Paris. A host of street performers normally provide entertainment. Only Notre Dame sees more tourists. The church is of relatively recent vintage, voted into being in 1873 by the National Assembly, but not completed until 1919. The white-stone Romano-Byzantine profile has been called the "whipped cream palace" by many. **Henry Miller**, while carousing seedy streets of Place Pigalle in the wee hours of 1936, said it was "like a white dream, like a dream imbedded in stone." The cloudlike poofs of the exterior give way to an interior gloomy by contrast, though certainly not cramped—it's about 320 feet by 250 feet, covered by a central dome 260 feet in the air. Prominent is a huge mosaic of Christ. Acoustics are fabulous, and choir performances and practices are frequent. The 275-foot campanile holds one of the world's largest bells, weighing 19 tons.

The church sits upon **Buttes Montmartre**, about 400 feet above the Seine (not quite the elevation of Belleville, in the 20th arrondissement). The hill is riddled, literally, with history. Tunnels from Gallo-Roman gypsum mines made the mount's ground unstable, and construction of the basilica began with the filling in of many of them with mortar and adding stabilizing archways. Montmartre (Mount of Martyrs) got its name in the mid-third century when Catholic Bishop **St. Denis** was beheaded here, along with two priests. The mount's history began centuries before that, when anthropologists believe religious stone megaliths were place by the **Druids**. In 1589, **Henry of Navarre** laid siege to Paris from the Montmartre, and then went on to become King Henry the IV. He converted to Catholicism. In 1814, Montmartre was the site of the losing battle against the Prussian-Russian alliance, the first army to invade Paris in 400 years. Another defeat at the hands of the Prussians in 1874 prompted the building of Sacre Coeur as a national repentance.

FACING THE CHURCH, PASS TO THE LEFT ON RUE CARDINAL GUIBERT AND THEN LEFT ON

RUE DE CHEVALIER DE LA BARRE. THEN GO LEFT ON RUE DU MONT CENIS TO PLACE DU TERTRE.

July 1 is a day of observance against religious oppression in Paris, memorializing **Chevalier de la Barre**, who was executed in 1766 by the Catholic church friars for "impiety"—the young knight was in possession of a book by Voltaire and was also whistling in a way that was deemed disrespectful. On the cobblestone street that bears his name you will have ample opportunity to be memorialized in a caricature by one of many sketch artists. You can also buy ice cream, a T-shirt, posters, and nifty beret.

The tourist action peaks at **Place du Tertre**, a fairly large square made intimate by open-air restaurants and an artist's bazaar that share its center. Some 140 licensed artists hawk portraits, kitsch landscapes, and silhouettes. Village shops and restaurants surround the *place*, which hums into the night. **Chez la Mere Catherine**, dates from 1793.

It's easy to overlook the hill's oldest church, **St. Pierre de Montmartre**, which is on the left as you enter the square. The first stone temple here was Roman, originally for sun worship and then dedicated to Mercury, the favored god of Gaul. Columns from the 7C remain on the west wall. The current edifice is essentially that of a 12C Benedictine Abbey, but a hodgepodge of styles has been added over the centuries. The façade is from the 17C, while the Romanesque nave was constructed in the 15C. The south aisle dates from 1838, while the bronze doors are spanking new, circa 1980. The church was where vows were taken that led to the founding of the **Society of Jesus**—the Jesuits—according to the earliest biography of Saint Ignatius Loyola.

TAKE A CLOCKWISE SWING AROUND PLACE DU TERTRE, AND THEN GO LEFT ON RUE NORVINS. FOLLOW TO RUE GIRARDON.

Detour: To take a side trip to the otherworldly world of artist **Salvador Dali**, leave Rue Norvins at the first left, on **Rue Poulbot**. At #11 is **Espace Dali** the subterranean museum with dreamy lighting cast upon more than 300 paintings, etchings, and sculptures. An admission is charged. Dali came to Paris at age 22 in 1926, fresh from being expelled from a famed art school in his native Spain. Fellow Spaniard Pablo Picasso was an early admirer. Though Dali's influences were as broad as the twentieth century, he is known as the Father of Surrealism—and for his flamboyant upturned moustache. He died in 1989, 15 years after an illness had robbed him of his gift.

Back on Rue Norvins, you will reach Rue Saules, an intersection known as **Utrillo's Corner**, since it was a favorite subject of Impressionist painter, Maurice Utrillo. Montmartre becomes rustic and more like a village, albeit a high-priced one, as you reach Rue Girardon. *Detour:* For a short side-trip that is long on character, go left on this street, and stay right at Rue Lepic. After a half-block, look up through a wooded park to see **Moulin de la Galette**—the best remaining example of some three-dozen windmills that once twirled on the butte, beginning in the 17C. The mills were used to crush corn, press grapes, and pulverize stone into construction material. But Galette was also a famous cabaret, dancehall, and way of life, captured in an 1898 painting by Renoir. Picasso and Van Gogh also painted the windmill.

FROM RUE NORVINS, GO STRAIGHT ACROSS GIRARDON TO AVE. JUNOT. TURN RIGHT INTO A SMALL PARK, SQUARE SUZANNE BUISSON.

RUE LEPIC

PIERROT
GOURMAND

MONTMARTRE

SACRE COEUR

PLACE DU TERTRE

WALK OUT THE OTHER SIDE OF THE SQUARE DOWN STAIRS TO PLACE CASADESSUS. GO RIGHT ON A WALKWAY (ALLEE DES BROUILLARDS) TO PLACE DALIDA.

On Junot you'll pass **Cine 13**, a chic theatre and dance venue. **Square Suzanne Buisson** is named for a WWII resistance fighter who was killed after saving her comrades. It is a restful green island surrounded by artfully-sited cottages and apartments. Nannies parade with kids in tow. The square's noted feature is a statue of **Bishop St. Denis**, holding his head, which he then carried to the site of his basilica in northern Paris. St. Denis introduced Catholicism to the city in the 3C, angering the then power elite.

FROM PLACE DALIDA, GO UPHILL ON RUE DE L'ABREUVOIR. GO LEFT ON RUE DES SAULES AND THEN RIGHT ON RUE SAINT VINCENT.

Where Rue de l'Abreuvoir meets Saules is **La Maison Rose** restaurant, pink through and through, the subject of a poem by Gertrude Stein and paintings by Pissarro and Utrillo. The restaurant offers simple French food at a reasonable price. A block away, on the right where Rue Saules meets Rue Saint Vincent, is the small acreage of **Vines de Montmartre**, producing grapes for about 1,000 bottles of decent wine yearly. A grape fete in October celebrates the corkage, and also the historic fact that this vineyard was one among those saved in 1929 when other vineyards went residential. But the big deal on this corner is across the street at **Le Lapin Agile**. The cozy, oft-photographed wine bar was the hangout for painters such as Picasso, Modigliani, Gauguin, Apollinaire, and others. At the turn of the twentieth century you could acquire one of their works for a bowl of soup and glass of wine. The sign, an agile rabbit jumping from a pan, dates from 1875. Now a thriving wine bar

that delivers an authentic experience, the restaurant once had rougher elements—anarchists, pimps, and rich students on a lark. The son of an early owner was murdered on site, and for a time it was called Café des Assassins.

FROM THE END TO ST. VINCENT, ENTER PARC DE LA TURLURE AND GO RIGHT UP THROUGH THE PARK, TURN RIGHT ON RUE DU CHEVALIER DE LA BARRE, AND FOLLOW TO THE FRONT PLAZA (PARVIS) OF SACRE COEUR.

Parc de la Turlure is on the site of a former mill. Today it hums with inactivity—bees in blossoming trees, a small waterfall beside flower beds, and quiet view benches under a vine-laced arbor. Tired tourists and young lovers take respite behind Sacre Coeur.

From the parvis in front of Sacre Coeur, facing away from the church, take stairs to the left, cross Rue Cardinal Dubois, and go left into **Square Louise Michel** and down the rustic **Maurice Utrillo stairs**. This hillside park was planted in 1927, and some exotic trees have diameters of 10 feet. The stairs swerve down to a wide pathway, across from which is the small square at **Rue Paul Albert**, an inviting cafe tableau. From the stairs, go right on the wide path, undulating through greenery to near the staircases of Sacre Coeur at the bottom. On the left across the street is the colorful, now-looking **Musee d'Art Naif Max Fourny**, opened in 1986 in Halle St. Pierre, a building dating from 1868. The museum displays folk art pieces and work by current artists.

GO LEFT DOWN THE STAIRS TO PLACE ST. PIERRE. GO LEFT, THEN VEER RIGHT ON RUE LIVINGSTONE. AFTER A BLOCK GO RIGHT ON RUE D'ORSEL (WHICH MERGES WITH RUE LIVINGSTONE). CONTINUE PAST TWO STREETS AND GO LEFT ON RUE DE STEINKERQUE AND CONTINUE TO RUE ROCHECHOUART.

PLACE DU TERTRE

PARC DE LA TURLURE

RUE PAUL ALBERT

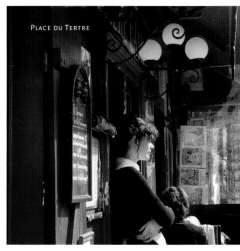

PLACE DU TERTRE

The tourist world of Montmartre drops quickly in the rear view on **Rue Livingstone**, which is a world of wholesale fabric. Bolts of every imaginable stripe and texture are heaped on shelves, stuffed in store windows, and piled on the sidewalk. If you want more, continue down Rue d'Orsel and double back. **Rue de Steinkerque** is a glittery garage sale of souvenirs, T-shirts, and trinkets, passed by a sea of visitors jabbering in multiple languages. The street offers the full frontal view of the great ice cream cone church on the hill.

IF YOU'VE HAD ENOUGH, END THE DAY AT THE ANVERS METRO STOP, LINE 2. TO CONTINUE ALONG A NEIGHBORHOOD MARKET STREET TO A GLORIOUS CHURCH, GO RIGHT, DOWN THE GREEN MEDIAN OF RUE ROCHECHOUART. IN TWO BLOCKS, GO LEFT ON RUE DES MARTYRS AND CONTINUE TO NOTRE DAME DE LORETTE. IT'S ALL DOWNHILL.

Impossible-to-pronounce **Rue Rochechouart** becomes **Boulevard de Clichy** at Rue des Martyrs. Along this now-busy corridor at the base of Montmartre were once the apartments and studios of the bulk of artists and writers—Toulouse Lautrec, Picasso, Degas, Dickens, George Sand, Emile Zola and many others. The prime era was from about 1890 to 1910.

Swerving downhill from Montmartre for a half-mile, **Rue des Martyrs** is a very livable neighborhood for young professional families as well as arty types (the French call it "bobo," for bohemian-bourgeois). Markets and street fairs amp the weekends. On Sundays the street is closed to cars. Martyrs is not as intense as the Left Bank, and not tourist-dominated. Antiques, art, and furniture stores mix with all the foodie options. At #39 is **Arnaud Delmontel**, featuring killer almond croissants and sought-after Renaissance bread. Vying for customers (and doing well) at #46 is **Rose Bakery**, where an oven is an artist's kiln. For nightlife, if you like jazz and world music, try **Le Divan du Monde** at #76.

Rue de Martyrs ends at the rear of notorious **Notre Dame de Lorette**. In the late 19C, this church was where mistresses living in the neighborhood would pray at pews nearby their suitors and family. All of this was above board and bourgeoisie—as depicted in newspaper caricatures. Consecrated in 1836, the church is intimate by Paris standards and tucked beside taller buildings. The interior packs a visual wallop, with polished marble columns, gilded paneled ceiling, and ornate floral decorations that set off huge religious stained glass works. On Wednesdays in the early afternoon, you can usually catch an organ recital.

END AT NOTRE DAME DE LORETTE METRO STOP, LINE 12.

NOTRE DAME DE LORETTE

WALKING TOUR TEN

POSTCARDS:

Passy ... Musee du Vin ... Maison de Balzac ... Maison de Radio France ... Statue de la Liberte ... Hector Guimard's Art Nouveau of Rue Fontaine ... Avenue Mozart ... Foundation Le Corbusier ... Village d'Auteuil ... Jardin des Serres ... Stade Rolland Garros

THUMBNAIL:

This tour follows the old road to Versailles through the upper-crust 16th arrondissement, known for its ornate Art Nouveau buildings—described as "architecture you can eat." The *quartier's* history is revealed at a cavern that is the museum of wine. Nearby, author Honore Balzac's country cottage is another vestige of quieter times. The last leg is through an appealing *village* for the rich and powerful, and then to the farthest reaches of the Metro to visit the city's most-underrated park and plant conservatory. Fashionable, exclusive, historic, and chic—say *bonjour* to the 16th.

BIG PICTURE:

Fewer tourists make their way to the upscale 16th. The arrondissement is long and narrow, with intitmate spaces, but also with boulevards made for high-speed urban hiking.

DISTANCE: 2.5 to 3.5 miles   TIME: 3 to 4.5 hours

RUE FONTAINE

PASSAGE DES EAUX

AVENUE DU PARC DE PASSY

NOTRE DAME D'AUTEUIL

SQUARE HENRI COLLET

JARDIN DES SERRES

HAUSSÉE DE LA MUETTE

JARDIN DES POÈTES

WALKING TOUR
Ten

START AT PASSY METRO STOP, LINE 6.

GO DOWN STAIRS (TOWARD THE RIVER) TO BELOW THE METRO TRACKS AND TURN RIGHT AT SQUARE ALBONI. THEN GO RIGHT ON RUE DES EAUX AND CONTINUE A BLOCK TO SQUARE CHARLES DICKENS.

The streets below the Metro in Passy were Marlin Brando's stomping grounds in the movie *Last Tango in Paris*. Tucked in the corner of Square Charles Dickens is **Musee du Vin**, the 15C wine cellars for the vineyards tended to by the monks of the Abbey of Passy. Ancient limestone quarries were used as cellars. Vines covered the hillside down to the Seine and the wine was favored by Louis XIII. Free tastings are offered to those who do lunch.

DOUBLE-BACK FROM THE MUSEUM AND GO RIGHT ON RUE CHARLES DICKENS, AND THEN IMMEDIATELY RIGHT UP FLIGHTS OF STAIRS ON PASSAGE DES EAUX. AT THE TOP, GO LEFT ON RUE RAYNOUARD.

THEN GO LEFT DOWN STAIRS AT AVE. DU PARC DE PASSY. AT THE PARK, GO RIGHT ON AVE. MARCEL PROUST. VEER RIGHT ON NARROW COBBLESTONED RUE BERTON. GO UP STAIRS TO YOUR RIGHT, AND THEN GO RIGHT ON RUE RAYNOUARD TO MAISON DE BALZAC.

Passage de Eaux was named in 1650 for a mineral hot springs that was here—before it went underground about a century later. With views toward the Seine and Tour Eiffel, **Rue Raynouard** is a preferred address for the well-heeled residents of the 16th Arrondissement. At #20 is the office for AFS (American Field Service), one of the world's largest volunteer organizations, which came to fame in WWI by supplying medical transport.

Parc de Passy is one of more than a dozen

greenspaces of Paris built alongside modern apartments. Its three-plus acres offer a playground and a walkway of arches adorned with copious flowers. The narrow cobblestones of **Rue Berton** are from the 18th century, when this was a boundary of the lands of two lords, Passy and Auteuil. Today its quaint curves are a sometimes setting for fashion-model photo shoots.

At #47 Raynouard is **Maison de Balzac**, a museum since 1949. Admission is free. Novelist **Honore de Balzac**, known for witty-but-dark social tales, fled in 1840 to this then-country cottage to escape bill collectors. He rented the three-story space using the false name, Madame de Breugnol. When touring the gardens (featuring a bust of the author) notice that Balzac could escape via a back gate to Rue Berton. Fueled by black coffee, he wrote from midnight until morning on novels such as *La Cousin Bette*. Prolific work notwithstanding, Balzac's spending outdistanced his income until he died in 1850. Many soon-to-be great writers who followed were influenced by Balzac. The intimate museum is full of personal items.

DOUBLE-BACK ON WIDE RAYNOUARD, CROSS RANELAGH, AND CONTINUE STRAIGHT ON TREED RUE FONTAINE.

At 51-55 Rue Raynouard is a building designed by 20C architect **Auguste Perret**, an early user of reinforced concrete, whose works emphasized "style without ornament." Largely scoffed at by his peers, the building now ironically houses the International Union of Architects. Farther down, at #68 (at the corner with Rue Singer) is the Hotel de Valentinois, which was the residence of **Benjamin Franklin** from 1777 to 1785, when he formed an alliance with Louis XVI and also cultivated a taste for Parisian life.

CASTEL BERANGER

MAISON DE BALZAC

ISLE OF SWANS

On the left after crossing Rue du Ranelagh the **Maison de Radio France**, a.k.a. The Round House, is home to nearly 100 studios for French public radio and television. It opened in 1963. A museum inside details electronic communications since the first crude telegraph in 1793. To run a mile, stop just short of four laps around the building's silvery walls. The expansive interior, the largest square footage of any building in France, is heated geothermally, utilizing a 600-meter deep bore-hole below the foundation.

The prevalence of Art Nouveau buildings increase at **Rue Fontaine**. On the right at #14 is **Castel Beranger**, a 36-unit apartment building that is the masterwork of the king of Art Nouveau, the Lyon-born architect Hector Guimard. Guimard is best known for the designs of 140 curving iron-and-glass Metro entrances between 1900 and 1904—only two of which remain. He landed that gig after the accolades heaped upon the Beranger building in 1898. After viewing the entry, with copper tufted like meringue, be sure to walk down the courtyard to take in the etched windows and stem-and-branch details of the compound. Critics take flight on the subject of Guimard and one called Beranger a "judicious mix of rational planning and non-rational intent and expression." At the time, many of Guimard's peers thought him "deranged."

IN FRONT OF CASTEL BERANGER, CROSS THE STREET, TAKE A WALKWAY THROUGH THE BUILDING AT #7, AND CONTINUE TO THE PARK OF SQUARE HENRI COLLET. GO RIGHT THROUGH THE PARK TO RUE GROS.

Detour: To see a smaller replica of the **Statue of Liberty**—set on the slender **Isle of Swans** in the Seine—go left on Rue Gros. At Place Clement Alder (Radio France is on the left) go right and cross the Seine on Pont de Grenelle. This version of Bartholdi's statue was presented to France by Americans, and placed on the island for the 1889 World Exposition. Note: Another way to visit the statue is to walk downriver on the island, on Allee des Cygnes (Swans). From the Bir Hakim Metro stop on Line 6, the closest stop to Tour Eiffel, head for the bridge and go down the stairs on your left.

FROM THE PARK, CROSS RUE GROS TO NARROW RUE AGAR, WHICH MAKES A RIGHT-ANGLE AND ENDS AT RUE FONTAINE. GO LEFT ON FONTAINE AND CONTINUE SEVERAL BLOCKS TO A PLACE WHERE AVE. MOZART JOINS FROM THE RIGHT AT AN ACUTE ANGLE. GO RIGHT ON MOZART, CROSS THE STREET, AND JOG RIGHT TO TINY RUE OLCHANSKI.

The cobbled alleyway of **Rue Agar** has several of **Guimard's** later facades, most completed around 1911. At #43 Rue Gros as you reach Rue Agar is one of his works. The addresses to look for on Rue Agar, which are noted by signs, are #4 on the corner, #8, #10, and #19. Back on **Rue Fontaine**, you'll find other works by Guimard at #21 and #19. A block later on the left is **Rue Fr. Millet**, an almost uniformly Art Nouveau block where you might want to do a down-and-back. Across Fontaine at Rue Millet is **Saint Therese**, a church of relatively new vintage with large parklike grounds.

Continuing down **Rue Fontaine** new buildings mix with older. Another 1911 effort by **Guimard** is **Hotel Mezzara** at #60. **Marcel Proust** was born at the home of his well-to-do uncle at #96. Much of the author's work was done while fighting lung diseases. Proust's 1.5-million word, several-volume novel, Remembrances of Things Past, was written mostly from his sickbed, over a 13-year span beginning in 1909.

Comma-shaped **Rue du Capitaine Olchanski** is a desirable address for Art Nouveau aficionados. And a half-block up Avenue Mozart, **Villa Flore**, is a set-piece from 1924, with curving brick and frosted glass set in decorative iron. At #122 Ave. Mozart is **Hotel Guimard**, the architect's residence, also dating from 1924.

Detour 1: **Avenue Mozart** is a main artery for those living the good life in the **16th Arrondissement**. One option to see more of it is to walk up Mozart two blocks to the Jasmin Metro and go two stops to the La Muette Metro, both on Line 9. **Chaussee de la Muette** is a trendy street of cafés that leads to **Jardin du Ranelagh**, a large neighborhood park with paths. The bistro **La Rotonde** is a people magnet.

Detour 2: **Foundation Le Corbusier**, which houses the museum **La Maison Roche,** is a few blocks away. The foundation honors Swiss-born architect Charles Edouard Jeanneret (1887-1965), an opinionated innovator of what became "modern urban architecture." After an initial stint in the offices of Auguste Perret, Jeanneret adopted the moniker, Le Corbusier. The modest museum—with curving walls, small rooms, and sleek lines—was built in 1923 for a Swiss art collector, although the artworks do not hang in the museum today. An admission is charged. To get there, walk up Mozart one block and go left up Rue Henri Heine for two blocks (passing an apartment by Guimard at #18). Then walk left on Rue du Docteur Blanche and left again onto quiet Square du Docteur Blanche.

DOUBLE-BACK ON BUSY AVE. MOZART, PASS RUE OLCHANSKI AND VEER RIGHT ON RUE POUSSIN. THEN GO LEFT ON RUE DONIZETTI AND CONTINUE TO RUE D'AUTEUIL.

On the right, as you turn left on Rue Donizetti, are the guarded gates of **Villa Montmorency**, an enclave of politicians, pop stars (like Celine Dion), and the type of multinational tycoons who don't want their addresses known. The upper 16th is home to rustic estates with nice gardens and armed security guards. The street life of the quarter, revolving around the intersection of **Rue d'Auteuil** and **Rue Michael Ange**, has all the fine things, but it's more down-to-earth than hoity. It dates from 1109, when the abbots of Saint Genevieve became the lords of **Auteuil**, which lasted 600 years. Auteuil was once a rural hamlet, known for healthful mineral hot springs, on the fringe of west Paris—and on the way to Versailles. In 1860 it was merged into Paris. Auteuil's quaint streets become the setting for the ritzy-cool scene created by the French Open tennis tournament.

Detour: Go left from Donizetti on Rue d'Auteuil to the village square at **Notre Dame d'Auteuil**. Though of recent vintage (1880s), this Roman-Byzantine church evokes the hamlet's past, especially when the bell rings from its 200-foot spire. Church organs in Paris are famous for different reasons, but those who know say this one delivers the truest sound. The obelisk in the *place* across from the church is the only remnant from a former cemetery.

CONTINUE ON RUE D'AUTEUIL (OR TAKE METRO ONE STOP) TO PLACE DE LA PORTE D'AUTEUIL. TAKE THE UNDERGROUND PEDESTRIAN WALKWAY. CROSS LEFT AT FOUNTAIN ONTO AVE. DU GENERAL SARRAIL. THEN WALK RIGHT INTO JARDIN DES POETES.

Traffic dominates the neighborhood at **Boulevard Peripherique**, the freeway that encircles Paris's 20 arrondissements. Visual peace returns inside the gates of

BERTON

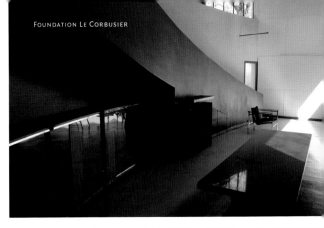
FOUNDATION LE CORBUSIER

JARDIN DU RANELAGH

PORTE D'AUTEUIL

JARDIN DES SERRES

Jardin des Poetes. Pick a garden path around the central lawn that is ringed with plaques honoring poets and statues, including a bust of Victor Hugo. Keep right and you will reach a gate and park plan for **Jardin des Serres d'Auteuil**. Here you will find a marriage of art, science, and nature: the 1761 botanical gardens by Louis XV. In 1898, five glass-and-wrought-iron greenhouses were built, arranged like palaces in a larger garden of seven acres. Serres by design blooms all year round, with plants from the Tropics, Japan, England, and the Mediterranean countries—palms, bananas, hibiscus, and several hundred other flowers and trees. Gardeners here, aside from tending to the glass houses and kempt grounds, produce yearly about 100,000 plants that are given homes in the public buildings of Paris.

When it opened, tickets to **Jardin des Serres** (serres means "glass houses") had to be rationed in the winter, since so many Parisians sought its ability to treat a variety of illnesses (too much wine among them). The gardens are still loved—but

not as much by everyone. Just across the street (Avenue Gordon Bennett) is **Stade Roland Garros**, built in 1928 to defend the Davis Cup in tennis and now the site of the French Open. Though a venue for one of the world's four Grand Slam tourneys, the stadium is by far the smallest, with less than half the capacity of Wimbledon. A plan is afoot to expand the tennis complex toward Jardin des Serres. The proposal ignited conflict among Paris's power elite, with everyone throwing stones. Tennis fans apparently have won the battle, and the stadium complex will expand into the gardens and create substantial changes over several phases, ending in 2015.

RETURN TO THE PORTE D'AUTEUIL METRO STOP, LINE 10. THIS METRO LINE HAS A ONE-WAY LOOP, SO YOU BEGIN BY TRAVELING AWAY FROM PARIS. EITHER GET OUT AT THE NEXT STOP (BOULOGNE JEAN JAURES) AND TAKE THE CAR ON THE OPPOSITE TRACKS, OR JUST GO TO THE END OF THE LINE AT BOULOGNE PONT DE SAINT CLOUD AND TAKE THE RETURN TRAIN TO PARIS.

Promenades

HALF-DAY WANDERINGS
MOSTLY IN THE OUTER
ARRONDISSEMENTS,
USUALLY BEGINNING AND
ENDING AT THE SAME
METRO STATION.

MUSEE RODIN

Promenade One

INVALIDES — MUSEE RODIN — RUE CLER MARKET

The masculine side of Paris resides at Invalides—a historic army hospital and museum that features the grandiose tomb of Emperor Napoleon. The spacious grounds are a tribute to military glory. And yet the city's feminine face is close by, at the mansion that houses the works of the sculptor Auguste Rodin, and at the market, where the subtleties of *gastronomie* are laid out as artwork.

START VARENNE METRO STOP, LINE 7

WALK AWAY FROM THE SEINE ON BLVD. DES INVALIDES (INVALIDES WILL BE ON YOUR RIGHT) AND MAKE THE FIRST LEFT, ON RUE DE VARENNE. MUSEE RODIN WILL BE ON YOUR RIGHT WITHIN ONE BLOCK.

Musee Rodin is housed in **Hotel Biron**, where the great sculptor essentially worked for rent for nine years until he died in 1908. The hotel began in 1730 as the home of the Duc de Biron, a general who was guillotined during the Revolution. Moving in next was the Duke of Maine, Louis XIV's illegitimate son, followed by the Catholic Church in the 1800s. The church established a boarding house. The French Government took over in 1910, allowing **Auguste Rodin** and other artists to stay in the house if they agreed to leave their works to the state in exchange. Dancer Isadora Duncan, the German poet Rainer Maria Rilke, and painter Henri Matisse were among other notable boarders.

The modestly appointed two-story mansion holds 500 of Rodin's smaller works as well as busts of Hugo and Balzac. One of Rodin's masterworks, *The Kiss*, is treasured. A number of paintings collected by Rodin adorn walls, including works by Van Gogh and Renoir. Sculptures by Rodin's apprentice **Camille Claudel** quiver in stone and threaten to steal the show. Be sure to see *The Age of Maturity* downstairs by the marble fireplace, which depicts Claudel's painful and ultimately destructive love triangle with Rodin and his lifetime lover. Admission is charged; free on the first Sunday of the month.

The museum is surrounded by a huge French formal garden anchored by a large circular pool. Paths meander through groves of broadleaf trees and many thoughtfully sited sculptures like *The Thinker, Balzac, The Gates of Hell,* and *Burghers of Calais*. The garden is a tranquil world apart from the massive Invalides just over the wall, and from the formality of **Rue de Varenne**, a run of staid classical mansions that house embassies and governmental ministries.

DOUBLE-BACK ON RUE DE VARENNE TO BLVD. DES INVALIDES AND GO LEFT. CROSS THE BOULEVARD AND GO RIGHT ON AVE. DE TOURVILLE.

EGLISE DU DOME

Paris, the city of art and fashion, shows its manly face at **Hotel des Invalides**. It was built in 1671 by Louis XIV as a royal hostel and hospital for disabled and retired soldiers. Invalides is now most famous as the resting place of Emperor Napoleon Bonaparte. From Avenue de Tourville, you approach gold-leafed **Eglise du Dome**, where France's famed warrior was laid to rest in a circular gallery in 1840—after the English agreed to return his body to France, 20 years after his death in St. Helena. He is fitted very safely inside of seven coffins-within-coffins. The innermost cask is iron, which is encased in mahogany, followed by two of lead, then ebony encased by oak, and finally the red porphyry outer sarcophagus. **Napoleon's Tomb** was completed in 1861. An admission is charged.

Pass to the right on the outside of Eglise du Dome and behind it you will find **Eglise Saint Louis**, a church for the patients that was built in 1861, the work of Jules Mansart (as is the Dome church). Behind Saint Louis is the **Cour d'Honneur**, the formal, symmetrical courtyard that lies within the massive, two-story stone buildings. Wide walkways encircle both levels, a classic design. Cannons, tanks, and antiquated armaments are placed in alcoves. As you enter the courtyard, you will want take a corner stairway to the second level to see a larger-than-life **statue of Napoleon**, which lords over the courtyard and the past. The beefy statue once topped the column at Place Vendome.

On the east side of the courtyard is the **Musee de l'Armee**, opened in 1905. Inside are racks in formation of colorful uniforms, surrounded by gleaming swords, daggers, armored suits, emblems, shields, and pistols. Military paraphernalia dates from antiquity to the twentieth century. All that's missing to start a war are the young men. At the far end of Cour d'Honneur are gilded gates that open to **Esplanade des Invalides**. Extending to the banks of the Seine, the 30-acre esplanade was laid out in 1720. It's undergone changes, but these days lime trees shade the benches and courts of boules players.

CROSS THE LAWN AND GARDEN FROM THE EXIT GATES TO PLACE DES INVALIDES. GO LEFT THROUGH PLACE DE SANTIAGO DU CHILE AND CROSS BLVD. DE LA TOUR MAUBOURG. CONTINUE STRAIGHT ON RUE DE GRENELLE FOR SEVERAL SHORT BLOCKS AND GO LEFT ON RUE CLER.

The wide, pedestrian-only cobblestones of **Rue Cler** are flanked by the epicurean delights of Paris, making it a darling among street markets, especially for American tourists and the upper-crust housewives of the 7th arrondissement. Even non-foodies will be amazed. Start with state-of-the art fruits and veggies at **Halles Bosquet** on the corner.

Swing into **Bacchus** (on the left) for the perfect bottle of wine, and then pull into **Davoli** for specialty meats—to call this place an Italian delicatessen is like calling the Mona Lisa a painting of a woman. For sweets, try **Le Mere de Famille Chocolats**, where traditional gourmet treats have been sold for decades. On the right before Rue Cler ends at Avenue de la Motte Picquet, look for **Olivier & Co**. and their quality olive oils, coveted among international celebrity chefs. Just about every doorway on this market street is worth a side trip. Build a picnic lunch or dinner and head for a nearby bench at Champs de Mars.

Rue Grenelle, on either side of Cler also has fine shops and cafes. Go north on Rue Cler one block to **Rue Saint Dominique** for more street shopping that defines the art of living in Paris. Christian Constant, a one-star Michelin chef, owns four excellent restaurants on this street: Cafe Constant at #139, Les Cocottes at #135, Le Violon d'Ingres at #137 and Les Fables de la Fontaine at #131. Try at least one. If you're in search of a Starbucks, duck in at #90 for a whiff of the U.S.A.

END AT THE ECOLE MILITAIRE METRO STOP, A BLOCK TO THE RIGHT FROM RUE CLER, ON AVE. DE LA MOTTE PICQUET AT PLACE DE L'ECOLE MILITAIRE.

Promenade Two

MONTPARNASSE

For a half-century—from about 1920 to 1970—this was the place on earth to be for writers, artists, and entertainers of every stripe. Some were already famous, from Montmartre, but thousands were American expatriates who followed the dreams of the "Lost Generation."

BEGIN AT THE VAVIN METRO STOP, LINE 4. EMERGE AT THE INTERSECTION OF BLVD. RASPAIL AND BLVD. MONTPARNASSE.

In the 17C, poets and students gathered on the rocky hills of "Montparnasse" (a tribute to the Greek Mount Parnassus) to read their works. The hills were leveled a century later when the boulevards were built, but the name remained and intellectualism began to peak. When Montmartre became too touristy for the artists and intelligentsia in the 1920s, they made an exodus across town to **Montparnasse**, along the border of the 6th and 14th arrondissements. They were joined by often-penniless painters and writers from everwhere. In three years beginning in 1921, American numbers swelled in Paris from six thousand to 30 thousand.

Creative juices centered at several cafes and brasseries. **La Rotonde**, on the corner of Montparnasse and Raspail, opened in 1911 and was a favorite of Picasso. Across Montparnasse at #108 is **Le Dome**, which opened in 1898. Among the "Domiers," as they were called, were Anais Nin, Henry Miller, Kadinsky, Man Ray, and Sinclair Lewis. The Dome's owners bought a coal and wood store a few doors down, at #102, and opened **La Coupole** (Little Dome) in 1927. Among other cultural icons to hold down chairs (and perhaps feast on a plate of cheap mashed potatoes and flutes of champagne) were Faulkner, Matisse, James Joyce, Josephine Baker, Ezra Pound, Samuel Beckett, Joan Miro, and Chagall. A long block away on the boulevard (at #171) is **La Closerie des Lilas**, which attracted the later stalwarts of the Lost Generation—Hemingway, Gertrude Stein, Alice B. Toklas, and Fitzgerald. Many great works of art came from sparking synapses and candlelit conversations along Boulevard Montparnasse. The cafe dates from 1847.

WALK UP BLVD. RASPAIL, CROSSING BLVD. MONTPARNASSE AND RUE DELAMBRE. TURN RIGHT ON RUE HUYGHENS AND CONTINUE TO BLVD. EDGAR QUINET.

The parklike median of **Boulevard Edgar Quinet** is the setting for one of the city's better outdoor markets—everything from seafood to scarves—on Wednesday and Saturday mornings. Across the boulevard from where Rue Huyghens joins Boulevard Quinet are the walls of **Cimetiere du Montparnasse** (an entry is at #3). The 45 treed acres were laid out in 1824, creating a little city of crypts and monuments for the departed, including a number of well-known Parisians. A map of the cemetery should be available at the entrance. Jean Paul Sartre and Simone de Beauvoir are to the right from the entrance. Actress Jean Seberg is straight ahead from the entrance, at a corner with the first major path. Novelist Guy de Maupassant is on the east side (to your left), off Rue Emile Richard, just past a monument to Baudelaire. A circle in the center of the grounds (Mount du Souvenir) is a good place to get oriented. Groundskeepers will be quick to volunteer directions.

EXIT THE CEMETERY TO BLVD. QUINET AND GO LEFT. CONTINUE, CROSSING RUE DE DEPART TO TOUR MONTPARNASSE.

Many of the monuments in Paris have been greeted with criticism (Tour Eiffel, Pompidou, Louvre pyramid) and then later embraced as magnificent. Such is not the case with **Tour Montparnasse**, which has been reviled by most Parisians since its construction in 1973. The 59-floor skyscraper has no twin in the cityscape, since planners moved that kind of architecture to La Defense (with artful results; see Promenade Eight, page 167). Still, for about 10 euros you can get a fabulous view of the city from a open-air terrace lofted at nearly 700 feet on the 56th floor.

EXIT TOUR MONTPARNASSE TO RUE DU DEPART.

To see a plaque commemorating where the **Germans surrendered** at the end of **WWII**, go left on Rue du Depart and cross Boulevard Montparnasse to Rue de Rennes. In 1944, a German general, knowing the war was lost, disobeyed a direct order from Hitler to destroy Paris, and instead extended the olive branch. To see **Gare Montparnasse**—and the sleek TGV trains that travel up to 200 mph—go right on Rue du Depart. The enormous station dates from 1840, but was overhauled in 1969 to accommodate the high-speed carriages. As a respite for travelers, an expansive garden, **Jardin Atlantique**, sits on the roof of the station. Paths swerve through willows and evergreens, home to songbirds. In a central lawn area is a large fountain (Fontaine

Hesperides), which mimics waves on the seashore, and also serves as a meteorological center. Built in 1994, the garden's nearly 9 acres are enclosed by other sleek office buildings—there is no view. To see the garden, take escalators and then stairs from the main foyer of the terminal. Or (easier) go to the back of the station at Boulevard Pasteur, and take a ramp up.

END MONTPARNASSE-BIENVENUE METRO STOP, LINES 4, 6, 12, 13.

Promenade Three
BERCY

With monumental views worthy of Paris and a modernity that manages to pay homage to the past, brand-new Bercy may well grow into its reputation of being the "New Left Bank." But to see its parks, plazas, and village you will need to walk both sides of the Seine.

START AT COUR ST. EMILION METRO STOP, LINE 14 (THE METEOR)

You will emerge from the metro near the corner of Rue de l'Ambroisie and Rue Francois Truffaut—near a small park hillock for newer upscale apartments. Walk down Truffaut and go left through Passage Saint Vivant into **Bercy Village**, a grid made up of some three-dozen stone former wine warehouses dating from the 19C. Metal roofs, glass gable ends, and the graphically sharp flags with the village logo give a modern uptake to this historic site. Shops cater more to residents than tourists: cafes, a pet store where Coco can get a coiffure, a cinema (the Truffaut connection), and a Monoprix market. Chocolates, Quiksilver surf duds, and microbrews are also at hand along the interior bricked space, called Cour Saint Emilion.

The old rail tracks in the bricks speak of **Bercy's** mainline linkage to the wine regions of France, when the village was outside the Paris city limits and therefore alcohol was tax-exempt. Newer transportation modes and incorporation into Paris in the early 1900s started a decline, and by 1970 most of the wine warehouses had been abandoned or destroyed. The village site is where flat-bottom boat relics from the Neolithic Period (6,500 years ago) were discovered, underscoring Bercy Village's theme of authenticity with a trendy façade.

BERCY VILLAGE

LEAVE THE VILLAGE VIA PASSAGE SAINT VIVANT, CROSS RUE TRUFFAUT, AND ENTER PARC DE BERCY.

The 31 acres of **Parc de Bercy** were the estate of a feudal lord in the 12C, before becoming Louis XIV's wine cellar in the 17C. The park, opened in 1994, is comprised of three large sections, beginning here with the **Romantic Garden**. Willows weep over a waterfowl-and-fish pond that surrounds a stone cottage on a small island. Visual tranquility rules. The water feature extends as a channel to the next park section.

PARC DE BERCY ROMANTIC GARDEN

Cross over Rue Joseph Kessel on one of the arched footbridges and enter the **Flowerbed** portion of the park. Paths zigzag through a rose garden, a bamboo mini-forest, and a community vegetable patch. The old brick-and-stone buildings were a farmhouse and orangerie. Flowerbeds are flanked by mature broadleaf trees. The intermingled details of the middle park give way to the wide-open lawns of the **Meadow**, a playground for Frisbee-loving dogs and green-seeking dwellers of the apartments that border the north side of the park. Benches rest under 100-year-old trees.

The large lawn lays below **Palais Omnisports de Paris Bercy POPB** , a 17,000-seat arena for indoor sports (tennis, basketball), concerts (Madonna, Springsteen), and "spectacles." Its steel-truss roof gives way to mountainous grassy banks that hide the building's structure and slope down to the lakelet and sculpted banks of the **Fontaine La Canyonaustrate**. Park goers can dip their toes in a faux-wild setting.

LEAVE THE PARK VIA THE WIDE STAIRS THAT ASCEND BY THE SKATEBOARD PARK—TO THE LEFT IN THE MEADOW AS YOU FACE THE SPORTS ARENA.

An elevated jogging path parallels busy Quai de Bercy, adorned here by a series of Asian-inspired totem sculptures. Cross the river on the fanciful **Passerelle Simone de Beauvoir**, a footbridge that undulates on several levels with a clear span of 350 feet. The footbridge was assembled in Alsace and voyaged via the North Sea, English Channel, and through narrow canals before being set in place at two in the morning in 2006. **Simone de Beauvoir** (1908-1986) was a philosopher and novelist, known also for her lifelong relationship with Jean Paul Sartre. Visible not far downriver along the Left Bank is **Piscine Josephine Baker**, a swimming pool floating on a barge with a retractable roof. Also sporting Jacuzzis, a fitness center, and wading pool, the facility can accommodate some 300 people.

But the grand view from the footbridge is of **Bibliotheque Nationale Francois Mitterrand**, beckoning Oz-like across the Seine. On each corner of a huge rectangular plaza are four,

PASSERELLE SIMONE DE BEAUVOIR

PISCINE
joséphine baker

20-plus-story towers, gleaming gold and L-shaped to mimic the shape of open books. The national library holds more than 10-million volumes, virtually everything published in France. Wide steps lead up to the plaza, comprised of about nine acres of hardwood decking. Beside the vast deck, presumably to make amends for the fallen forest, is a sunken pine grove, another acre-plus with several species of good-sized conifers. The book fortress opened in 1998. Several floors are open to the public, and reading rooms absorb scholars from around the globe.

ON THE OTHER SIDE OF BIBLIOTHEQUE NATIONALE IS AVENUE DE FRANCE. GO LEFT TWO BLOCKS TO A METRO STATION THAT ACCESSES LINE 14 (THE METEOR) AS WELL AS LINE C OF THE RER.

Promenade Four

CIMETIERE du PERE LACHAISE

The most exclusive address for a million former Parisians is this cemetery, the city's largest greenspace within the Boulevard Peripherique. It receives two million visitors each year from among the living.

START AT THE PHILIPPE AUGUST METRO, LINE 2.

The main entrance to **Cimetiere du Pere Lachaise** is on your right, about a half-block from the Metro station on Boulevard de Menilmontant. A map should be available at the main gate (or at the nearest tobacco stand), although even with one, navigating the 109-acre grounds is not easy. Dirt paths and cobblestone walkways weave through 100,000 ornate tombs and mossy headstones. The hillside is covered with a mature forest of chestnuts and other broadleafs. In the 17C, the property was the estate of **Pere Lachaise**, a priest whose ears heard the confessions of Louis XIV.

With grave space at a premium in central Paris, the government bought the estate in 1804. But during the next 13 years, only 2,000 plots were purchased. At that time a marketing whiz decided to move the remains of **Moliere** here. During the next ten years, 30,000 tombs were sold and since then Pere Lachaise has been called "the grandest address in Paris." About ninety percent of the graves are anonymous, and, with space a premium, old graves that have not

seen visitors for years are dug up to make room for the new. Throughout the cemetery, wealthy families have one-upped each other with their funerary art. Cats roam, black ones mainly.

ENTER THE CEMETERY FROM THE MAIN ENTRANCE ON AVENUE DE MENILMONTANT.

Go straight on Avenue Principale to the first crossing and to the left is the tomb of **Colette**, and not far from her is **Baron Haussmann**. Continue straight and go right on Avenue de la Chapelle. Continue to a circle, **Carrefour du Grand Rond**—where you are not far from **Frederic Chopin**. To find **Jim Morrison**, go around the circle and veer right. Graffiti sometimes points the way to the rider on the storm.

Double-back to the carrefour. Head to the right through the maze (going away from the entrance) to **Chemin Moliere**, where you can go right to find the grave of France's Shakespeare. The route curves, becoming Chemin Chamille Jordan, off of which is the monument to **Victor Hugo**. To pay your respects to **Edith Piaf**, make your way toward the southern wall and then go left on Avenue Transversale No. 2. Go left, and the songbird will be on your right.

In this northeast corner of cemetery is **Mur des Federes** (Federalist's Wall), where in 1871 some of the remaining Communards, 147 of them, were stood against the wall and shot. The mass execution was retaliation for the killing of an archbishop, and to stomp out the short-lived government that had taken over after the Franco-Prussian War. The Communards were buried in an open ditch. It is said a few survived, and hid out in Pere Lachaise by day and foraged for food from sympathizers outside the walls at night. Near this site are also shrines to the French Resistance of WWII, and to those who died in Nazi camps.

Continue on Tranversale and on the right (Avenue Pacthod) you will find the graves of **Gertrude Stein** and **Alice B. Toklas**. Then, farther along Transversale, go right on Avenue Carrette and you will find the neo-Egyptian tomb of **Oscar Wilde**. He took residence in 1910, a decade after his death. At Avenue Aquado, the next major path after Carrette, is the Columbarium et Crematoire. Around or near this large square are the monuments for **Isadora Duncan, Sarah Bernhardt, Simone Signoret,** and **Marcel Proust**.

EXIT THE CEMETERY AT THE NORTH END OF THE CREMATORIUM, ON AVE. DES COMBATTANTS ETRANGERS. CONTINUE ON AVE. DE PERE LACHAISE TO THE GAMBETTA METRO, LINE 3. (OR GO WEST BACK TO THE MAIN ENTRANCE AND USE THE PHILIPPE AUGUSTE METRO.)

Promenade Five

PARC DE LA VILLETTE

A huge urban "Tomorrow Land" on the outskirts draws ten million visitors each year—about the same number as the Eiffel Tower—many of them Parisians who are not trying to escape the bustle of the city.

START AT THE PORTE DE PANTIN METRO, LINE 5.

Large city parks, including Paris's most notable, exist to inject the soothing elements of nature into populated settings. But **Parc de la Villette** instead uses the elements of urban architecture and makes them playful. Ten themed gardens, 35 architectural follies, footbridges, and a fantastical science museum cover 125 acres that are cleaved by the **Canal de l'Ourcq**—all of it a play land for both kids and parents. The grounds were a slaughterhouse for a century until closing in 1974. The park opened in 1987 after receiving competing concepts from more than 400 architects (Bernard Tschumi won).

Cite de la Musique—to the right from the entrance near the Porte de Pantin Metro—is a venue for headliner performers and the site of a far-reaching music museum. From here you'll want to follow your whims on a swerving stroll through the park—there's not meant to be any symmetry to the place. A map is available at park offices—to the left of the **Fontaine aux Lions**, which adorns the opening place. Near the offices is the cinema that holds an international film festival, which has hosted the likes of **Sophia Coppola** and **Woody Allen**. From there, stay left of the large **Grande Halle** (a convention center) and follow the wavy walkway to reach the **Garden of Mirrors** and others with theme elements (dunes, wind, fog) that mingle with plant life.

CANAL DE L'OURCQ

GARDEN OF MIRRORS

Boat rides and bike rentals are available at the canal, which flows to Canal St. Martin and then the Seine. Bridges and elevated walkways afford different angles on the waterway. Not far away are the **Garden of Trellises** and the **Bamboo Garden**, both of which are on multiple levels and connected by ramps and bridges. Throughout Villette you will notice the red-enamel structures—follies—which are structures that look functional, but in this case are art-modern play sets. **La Trabendo**, a 700-seat club for jazz and other performers is near this (east) area of the canal. Wide spaces separate the signed attractions, letting visitors decide where to go next—part of Villette's theme of asking visitors for activity and interaction.

CITE DES SCIENCES

At the far end of the park is its main draw, **Cite des Sciences et de l'Industrie**, a rather drab name for a fun learning museum. The signature for Villette sits in front of the museum, **The Geode**, a mirror-clad, 100-foot-diameter geodesic dome that houses an IMAX theater. Next to that is the **Argonaute**, a beached black submarine that sits in a lake-sized moat that is filled by 10-foot-high waterfalls cascading from five incoming aqueducts. The inside of the museum is a cavernous space, made possible by exposed steel truss-beams and cable struts, so large that it takes awhile to pick out significant details, like a helicopter dangling in one section.

Busloads of schoolchildren are absorbed and entertained by interactive exhibits on volcanoes, the ocean, galaxies, and others that illustrate careers in the sciences. You'll want to see **La Serres**, which have been called a "bioclimatic façade," made up of three, 60-foot-high greenhouses that are built of structural glass—with no framing supports. Cite des Sciences is the largest science museum in Europe.

END AT THE PORTE DE LA VILLETTE METRO, LINE 7. TO GET THERE, EXIT PARC DE LA VILLETTE ON THE SIDE OF THE MUSEUM OPPOSITE THE GEODE AND THEN CROSS THE ESPLANADE DE LA ROTONDE TO THE STATION.

Promenade Six

MARCHE LES PUCES ST. OUEN

Need a T-shirt or knock-off designer watch? Looking to authentically furnish and decorate a faux chateau and have it all shipped to Santa Barbara?

START AT THE PORTE DE CLIGNANCOURT METRO STOP, END OF LINE 4.

The **Marche Puces St. Ouen** originated with enterprising "rag-pickers" in 1885, who laid out their scavenged wares for sale near the Porte de Clignancourt. More reverently called "moon fishermen," these street salesmen over the years built storefronts in alleyways and cubicles in warehouses. Les Puces today is largest flea market-slash-antique store in the world, with 3,500 licensed vendors set up on some 20 jammed-packed city acres. Every weekend, about a quarter-million people bring their cash, credit cards, and bargaining skills. Expect a crowded Metro car, and keep a wary eye on your valuables. Most stalls open at 9 on Saturdays, 10 on Sundays, and 11 on Mondays, with a closing time of around 6 everyday.

FROM THE METRO, WALK UP AVENUE DE LA PORTE DE CLIGNANCOURT, CROSS UNDER BLVD.
PERIPHERIQUE (THE FREEWAY), AND GO LEFT ALONG THE SHOP STALLS ON RUE JEAN HENRI FABRE.
AFTER A BLOCK, GO RIGHT INTO LES HALLES DAUPHINE.

Most visitors will want to pass by the table-loads of standard flea-market offerings (jeans,
sneakers, electronics, handbags) on the hectic outskirts of the market, set in a poorer French-
African neighborhood. After this initial street scene, **Marche Dauphine** will seem peaceful.
About 300 shops along dozens of signed walkways are enclosed by a brightly sky-lit, two-story
building. Unveiled only recently (1991), Dauphine's commerce revolves around a central
interior square, with palm trees and a fountain. The market defines eclectic, with jewelry, vases,
hookahs, marble mantles, nautical brass works, wood-carved boxes, and oodles of objets d'art.
But an overriding theme is printed works. Scattered about, you'll find movie posters, vinyl
records, maps, vintage books, prints and paintings, historic newspapers, old magazines, and
fine-art photographs (including some Man Rays).

EXIT MARCHE DAUPHINE OPPOSITE FROM WHERE YOU ENTERED. YOU'LL COME OUT AT #140 RUE
DES ROSIERS, ACROSS FROM RUE VOLTAIRE. CROSS ROSIERS, JOG LEFT, AND THEN GO RIGHT INTO
MARCHE BIRON, AT #85 RUE DES ROSIERS.

Marche Biron, set along two parallel, open-air alleys, has provided one-stop shopping for
finer homes since it opened in 1925. The right side (Alee 1) has many ornate, gilded furnishings
from the mid-1700s. The left side (Alee 2) draws most of the action. A red carpet runs under a
corrugated metal roof and is illuminated by a string of bulbs. Along this faux street, dozens of
open shops are decorated as rooms—studies, libraries, salons, dining rooms—giving the affect
of a long series of movie sets. Chandeliers, gold plates, ivory carvings, glassware, and paintings
are impeccably placed amid antique furniture settings, many of carved wood. Biron typically
has the most expensive wares.

AT THE FAR END OF MARCHE BIRON, JOG RIGHT AT AN ALLEY (GAGIN), AND THEN GO RIGHT AT A
MAIN STREET, WHICH IS AVENUE MICHELET. CONTINUE TO RUE VOLTAIRE AND THEN GO RIGHT INTO
MARCHE VERNAISON.

Along **Avenue Michelet** are street stands with more jeans and sweatshirts, mixed in with tourist
trinkets and junk, some of which rises to the level of antiques. **Marche Vernaison** is an antique
village unto itself, with 300 stalls placed along winding pathways so narrow that opposite
shop awnings nearly touch. Its several acres are triangle shaped, formed within the streets of
Michelet, Rosiers, and Voltaire. Although larger furniture pieces are available, Vernaison is
more heaped with smaller objects—toys, beads, decorative frills, jewelry, hair brushes, linens,

quirky utensils—and for that reason is the likely place for tourists to find a keepsake that can fit in a suitcase. Good manners are expected, but flea-market bartering takes place without pretense. Taking photos is frowned upon by some. During the first two weeks of August, many shopkeepers close and head south on vacation.

EXIT MARCHE VERNAISON ON THE SIDE OPPOSITE FROM WHICH YOU ENTERED, COMING OUT AT RUE DES ROSIERS.

To see several shops and smaller markets, take a further stroll along the main drag, **Rue des Rosiers**. Art Deco works and Asian furniture are among the goods offered at **Marche Antica**, at address #99. **Marche Cambo** (located in a warehouse) has about 20 vendors, selling mainly furniture. Cambo is at #75, just past Marche Biron.

On the opposite side of Rosiers are **Marche Serpette** at #110, and **Marche Paul Bert** at #96. The breadth of goods at these markets has drawn the attention of wealthy shoppers like the Gates family from Seattle, who buy by the boatload. Kitchenwares, hand-forged hardware, antique wall hangers, and the like are mixed with shops offering larger items, like dressers, stuffed armchairs, and ornately framed mirrors. More modern collections from the 1960s are also available for bidding. You'll also find an excellent assortment of prints and paintings.

As you walk back toward the Peripherique, look for **Marche Malassis** (at address #142); their goods are a feast for the eyes. The market has furniture from the 18C on, but the real treats are the silver pieces and museum-quality Asian works. About 100 shops, galleries, and boutiques are stacked on two floors, with a timespan of offerings from antiquity to kitsch.

Of course, all of the above, while exhausting, is not an exhaustive inventory of shops and storefronts of Marche aux Puces. Willful shoppers will find more and more... and more.

When it's time for a break, several restaurants have hearty French fare and plenty of atmosphere. Chez Louisette, 130 Avenue Michelet; La Pericole, 16 Rue Plaisir; and Rue des Rosiers establishments, Le Biron at #85, Les Terrases de Cayenne at #142 and La Chope des Puces at #122, where on Saturday and Sunday from 4 to 7 you can hear Django (gypsy jazz) music.

RETRACE YOUR ROUTE BACK DOWN AVENUE DE LA PORTE DE CLIGNANCOURT TO THE METRO

Promenade Seven
PARC de MONCEAU

To see how the gentry of Paris spent weekend leisure time in the nineteenth century, take a visit to Parc de Monceau today.

START AT THE MONCEAU METRO STOP, LINE 2.

Longing for a sublime oasis for relaxation in 1769, **Duke Philippe d'Orleans** (Philippe Egalite) bought about 40 acres at the village of Monceau. He commissioned a designer to create a country cottage surrounded by a wistful park in the rambling, wild English style—as opposed to the formal symmetry of other parks of Paris, like Luxembourg, and the Tuileries. At the time he was a cousin to the king, perhaps the richest man in France, and a man known to rejoice in his pleasures. The duke's full vision was halted in 1793 when he met the guillotine during the Revolution. But in 1860 the City of Paris bought the land and, under the guidance of Napoleon III's master planner Baron Haussmann, Parc de Monceau took the form it retains today—although it was halved in size to make room for ornate gated mansions that were typical of the period. As usual throughout Paris, Haussmann was aided by garden architect Jean Charles Alphand and by Gabriel Davioud, designer of ironwooks and fountains

ENTER THE PARK AT THE GILDED GATES AND ROTUNDA OFF BLVD. DE COURCELLES.

The **Rotonde de Chartres** at the entrance is an original structure enhanced by Haussmann. The building serves the practical purpose of housing a watchman of the park's four monumental gates, which are closed from sunset to sunrise. Residents of the six mansions that ring Monceau have access 24/7. On weekends and holidays, the park is full of people, most of whom (joggers and kids-gone-wild at the playground excepted) are intent on sitting or strolling while conversing. A path encircles the forested oval, and several others crisscross a gentle gardenscape.

You may wish to begin to the left on a clockwise amble. You will quickly encounter Monceau's amorphous pond, which is rimmed by a **Corinthian Colonnade**, one of several architectural follies in Monceau's original design. Others include an Egyptian pyramid, Dutch windmill, and a Renaissance arcade from the old **Hotel de Ville** (gone are a former Italian vineyard and Turkish minaret). Footbridges and a grotto add to the whimsy. A half-dozen monuments to great writers and musicians were added during the Belle Époque when this end of the Champs Elysee became fashionable. (**Guy de Maupassant's** tribute is near the pond and **Frederic Chopin's** is on the western end behind the playground.)

In spring, tulips and magnolias add romance to the gardens, as do languid willows near the pond. Grassy hills, pine trees, and mature broadleafs give dimension to the space. All of this may seem like an Impressionist painting, as it did to **Claude Monet**, who brushed three works here from 1876 to 1878.

When leaving Parc de Monceau, you may wish to consider two options (other than the rotunda gate):

ALTERNATIVE ONE: EXIT VIA THE WEST GATE AT AVE. VAN DYCK.

The courtyard at the formidable **Van Dyck gate** is surround by mansions of the period. Of particular note, at #5, is the **Hotel Emile Menier**, built by a man who parlayed his chocolate business into a sweet fortune and a place on the social register. Van Dyck extends a block to **Avenue Hoche**, a high-society street that was a private road in the early 19C. A 20-minute walk down Hoche gets you to the Arc de Triomphe, where 12 avenues converge at **Etoile** (The Star, formally Place Charles de Gaulle).

ALTERNATIVE TWO: EXIT VIA THE EAST GATE AT AVE. VELASQUEZ.

One of the most sumptuous mansions of the period—modeled after the Petit Trianon in Versailles—is now the **Musee Nissim de Camondo**, not far from the Avenue Velaquez gate. An admission is charged. To get there from Velasquez, go right on Boulevard Malesherbes and right again on Rue de Monceau to address #63. The estate was built in 1911 by an industrialist and banker, Moise Camondo, to house his large collection of 18C furniture and art objects. Opened in 1935, the museum is dedicated to Camondo's son who was killed in WWI. The family faced further suffering at the hands of the Nazis in WWII, showing that wealth is no safeguard against tragedy.

On the way out of the park (before Camondo) you will pass **Musee Cernuschi**, at 7 Avenue Velasquez. Holding more than 12,000 works of Asian art, this museum dates from 1898. For the Metro, double-back on Malesherbes to Avenue Courcelles and go left to the Monceau station.

END AT THE MONCEAU METRO STOP, LINE 2. IF YOU CHOOSE TO WALK AVE. HOCH, END AT CHARLES DE GAULLE-ETOILE METRO STOP, LINES 1, 2, 5, AND 6

Promenade Eight
LA DEFENSE

This mammoth forest of glass-and-steel skyscrapers leaves no doubt that France is a 21st-century multinational superpower—but one that is remains decidedly French.

START AT THE GRAND ARCHE DE LA DEFENSE METRO STOP, LINE 1. (DON'T EXIT AT ESPLANADE DE LA DEFENSE STOP.)

The headliner at La Defense is **La Grande Arche**, a futuristic send-up of the Arc de Triomphe, shaped like a hollowed-out cube more than 100 meters on a side. The center opening is large enough to easily provide a garage for Notre Dame. The building heads **Le Parvis la Defense**, the huge plaza that provides breathing room for pedestrians in the 80-acre complex. The parvis is surrounded by 14 of the 16 tallest structures in Paris, all of them architecturally sleek and formidable. The Grande Arche is one end of the **Axis Historique**, the 6-mile alignment that pierces Arch de Triomphe, continues down the Champs Elysees, and goes straight through the pyramid to end at the Louvre. The glass-and-Carrara-marble cube was completed in 1989. Until a minor elevator mishap occurred in 2010, visitors could enjoy an open elevator ride to the top floor restaurant and computer museum. The top floor is now closed to the public.

The **Grande Arche** complex is surrounded by 400 acres of greater La Defense with 72 buildings housing a quarter-million workers—the largest corporate complex in Europe. All of it stands where, 15 centuries ago, St. Genevieve, the patron saint of Paris, tended sheep as a child (circa 435 AD). The locale is also where in 1871 French soldiers made a stand against the Prussians (from which the entire complex takes it name). The area was a hodgepodge of smaller factories and decrepit outbuildings in 1958 when the project's first tower, the Esso building, rose from the ground. Momentum for more skyscrapers came in the 1970s after Tour Montparnasse showed how ghastly high-rises would be if included in historic Paris. Some 10 more towers are to be erected by 2016, but none taller than the Eiffel Tower.

Though overwhelming in scale and corporate might, La Defense manages to be people-friendly. The parvis (plaza) is fringed by retail stores and restaurants that draw trainloads of teens. The vast space is decorated by 60 sculptures, including a large Alexander Calder, and several fountains, including a music-synchronized water cannon. On Bastille Day 1990, La Defense hosted a concert that drew two million spectators, the largest such gathering on record.

ISLE DE LA GRANDE JATTE

EXIT VIA THE GRAND ARCH DE LA DEFENSE METRO. TO COMPLETE A LA DEFENSE EXPERIENCE, GET OUT AT THE PONT DE NEUILLY STOP, JUST ACROSS THE RIVER.

The metro crosses **Pont de Neuilly** with an open-air view of **Ile de la Grande Jatte**, once part of the sylvan estate of Louis Philippe Egalite. In 1773, the future king built a footbridge and added the **Temple of Love** on the tip of the island. It's a 20-minute round trip walk from the Metro. The bridge lured Van Gogh, Monet, Seurat, and other Impressionists. The **Neuilly Sur Seine Plaza** and fountain is right next to the Metro. With a short walk to the high point comes a view down Avenue Charles de Gaulle of the Arch de Triomphe and a bookend look at the Grande Arche.

END AT THE PONT DE NEUILLY METRO STOP.

Promenade Nine

PARC DE BAGATELLE

This park-within-a-park wooed Marie Antoinette with its formal gardens and floral array. Today, Bagatelle is a fast getaway to the slow pace of the countryside.

START AT THE PORTE MAILLOT METRO, LINE 1. FROM THERE TAKE BUS #244 DOWN ALLEE DE LONGCHAMP. THE PARK ENTRANCE IS A SHORT WALK FROM THE BUS STOP.

Parc de Bagatelle was a rustic hunting lodge in 1777 when Comte d'Artois, the brother of Louis XVI, bought the property. His sister-in-law, Marie Antoinette, never one for delayed gratification, goaded him into betting that a park and chateau could be built within three months. Nearly 1,000 workers, supervised by architect Francois Joseph Belanger, toiled day and night (using torchlights and serenaded by music) and the neoclassical **Chateau de Bagatelle**, along with an orangerie, an Asian-style pagoda, and other buildings were finished in 64 days.

What the queen lost on the bet is uncertain. She and the king did attend an extravagant inaugural fete, at which a new game was introduced—*bagatelle*. The game, which involved striking small ivory balls up a table with a bumper edges through obstacle pins, became popular throughout Europe and evolved to become the pinball machine. But by the end of the century, a new contraption called the guillotine became all the rage in Paris, putting an end to court life. (Comte d'Artois survived the Revolution and ascended to the thrown in 1824 as **Charles X**, but abdicated to keep his head six years later during the revolution of 1830.)

Though not small—at 59 acres it is larger than Jardin de Luxembourg— Bagatelle is less than five percent of the land of **Bois de Boulogne**, which surrounds it. Boulogne is 2.5 times larger than New York's Central Park. During the three years after the bet, gardeners added water features and winding paths, which were inspired by Parc Monceau. After the City of Paris purchased the grounds in 1905, horticulturalist Jean Claud Forestier developed flower gardens, including the **Roseraie**, which now includes 9,000-plus species and since 1907 has hosted to a yearly international competition to produce new rose species. The rose garden is to your left from the entrance. Waving fields of irises, daffodils, and peonies also contribute to three-season color at this well-tended oasis.

On the way to the rose garden is the **Orangerie Bagatelle**, set at the head of a formal garden with expansive lawns and benches. The orangerie each summer hosts the **Festival de Chopin**. The park's idyllic grotto, waterfalls, and pond are to the right from the main entrance. Water lilies and other aquatic plants—a tribute to Claude Monet—share the water with black swans, while peacocks and geese bob the shoreline and perhaps dare to walk one of the footbridges. Straight across from the main entrance (at the west entrance to the walled park) is the **Restaurant Bagatelle**, set on the grounds of the former redbrick stables, where you can dig deep into the wallet to enjoy a gourmet meal al fresco.

END BY TAKING THE #244 BUS BACK TO THE PORTE MAILLOT METRO STOP, LINE 1.

Promenade Ten

DOMAINE NATIONAL de SAINT CLOUD

After the royal estate of Chateau St. Cloud burned in 1870—the result of French artillery fire—the war with Prussia was lost and France would never again be ruled by a monarch.

START AT THE BOULOGNE-PONT DE ST. CLOUD METRO, LINE 10 (*not* PORTE DE SAINT CLOUD METRO, LINE 9). THE NATIONAL PARK IS ABOUT A 15-MINUTE WALK FROM THE METRO. WALK UP (TOWARD THE SEINE) AVE. MAR DE LATTRE DE TASSIGNY AND CROSS BUSY QUAI ALPHONSE DE GALLO. CROSS THE RIVER ON PONTE DE ST. CLOUD AND USE CROSSWALKS TO GO LEFT AND DROP LEFT ON A PEDESTRIAN ACCESS TO A LARGE PARKING LOT, WHICH IS THE EAST ENTRANCE OF THE PARK.

The 1,200 historic acres rising from the banks of the Seine were made a national park in 1994, **Domaine National de Saint Cloud**. A fancy hunting estate was built here in 1571, but the land was regally developed in 1658 when acquired by **Philippe duc d'Orleans**, the flamboyant younger brother of **Louis XIV, the Sun King. Chateau de Saint Cloud** grew to a magnificent estate, as its gardens were rebuilt during thte 1660s by **Andre le Notre** (1613-1700). The famed landscape architect also designed works at Versailles, Fontainebleau, and Chantilly.

In 1780, **Marie Antoinette** took a fancy, and expanded the chateau into a U-shaped palace that opened to a long view of Paris. Today's rose garden owes its start to the queen. **Emperor Napoleon Bonaparte** used the high ground of Saint Cloud as his principal residence and hunting lodge. Napoleon III (Bonaparte's nephew) also favored Saint Cloud, and from here declared an ill-fated war on Prussia. The Prussians captured the chateau in 1870 and laid siege to Paris. France returned cannon fire that inadvertently destroyed the chateau along with France's imperialist dreams. The chateau was razed in 1892. Restoration work continues on the grounds, which include a number of formal gardens, statues, and the most ornate fountain in France.

FROM THE PARKING LOT, WALK ACROSS THE OPEN FIELD (PARALLELING THE RIVER).

At the far end of the clearing is a massive, drably named statue, **France Crowning Art and Industry**, which was moved here in 1900 from the Universal Exposition at Trocadero.

DOUBLE BACK FROM THE STATUE TO THE CENTRAL FOUNTAIN. FOLLOW PATH ON LEFT TO THE TOP.

La Grande Cascade is a fabulously complex, gravity-fed fountain, with water tumbling down several wide terraces in multiple channels and spurting heads, the entirety decorated with sea creatures, masks, and baroque figures. A very long basin pool at the bottom tranquilizes the downpour. It was completed in several phases during the late 17C. The east terrace of the formal gardens, **Patio de los Narjonos**, is ringed by balustrades with panoramic river views. Near the other end of the of the terrace is a jetted circular fountain.

Down and to the left of the formal gardens is a sub-garden with several fountain pools and statuary. In succession along a tree-shaded slope are **Three Broths Basin**, **Dog Basin** (where large royal canines stand alert), and then **Avenue of the Water Chutes**. Most of the Domaine de Saint Cloud extends west from here into woodlands that are accessible from five country lanes extending from a central round fountain (**the Great Wave**). Walkers will want to turn back and go left onto one of the pathways to the top of the escarpment.

The high ground of the park is **Jardin de Trocadero**, featuring a small lake that is habitat for waterfowl and releases its outflow to feed the fountains below. Tall pines, cypress, and flowering trees border a rambling English-style shrub-and-flower garden. Upon this rise is another entrance to the park, as well as the **Musee du Chateau de Saint Cloud**. From this apex is a far-off view of Paris called "La Lanterne," because Napoleon would light a lantern here that was visible in Paris, letting the people know the emperor was in residence.

During wintry days, Parc de Saint Cloud can be a bittersweet, if not bleak monument to faded glory. In the summer during eclectic rock concerts—or once a year when the fountains come alive with rushing white water—the place is a tribute to art and nature everlasting.

END BY RETRACING YOUR PATH BACK TO THE BOULOGNE-PONT DE ST. CLOUD METRO STOP, LINE 10

DIAMOND VALLEY COMPANY, publishers

89 Lower Manzanita Drive, Markleeville, CA 96120
e-mail: trailblazertravelbooks@gmail.com

NO WORRIES PARIS, A photographic walking guide

GOLDEN GATE TRAILBLAZER, Where to hike, bike and walk in San Francisco and Marin

ALPINE SIERRA TRAILBLAZER, Where to hike, bike, ski, fish, drive from Tahoe to Yosemite

KAUAI TRAILBLAZER, Where to hike, bike, paddle, surf

OAHU TRAILBLAZER, Where to hike, snorkel, surf from Waikiki to the North Shore

MAUI TRAILBLAZER, Where to hike, snorkel, surf, drive

HAWAII THE BIG ISLAND TRAILBLAZER, Where to hike, snorkel, surf, bike, drive

NO WORRIES HAWAII, A vacation planning guide for Kauai, Oahu, Maui and the Big Island

Thank you for your readership!
To order go to www.trailblazertravelbooks.com,
amazon.com, barnesandnoble.com, powells.com